D0626806

Theories of Cognitive Development

Theories of Cognitive Development:

Implications for the Mentally Retarded

Edited by

ROBERT M. ALLEN

ARNOLD D. CORTAZZO

RICHARD P. TOISTER

University of Miami Press
Coral Gables, Florida

Library of Congress Catalog Card Number 72-92899

ISBN 0-87024-249-0

Designed by Bernard Lipsky

Manufactured in the United States of America

Contents

Foreword 7

Preface 9

I Why Retarded Children Do Not Perform Up to the Level of Their Ability 13
Edward Zigler

II The Transactional Approach in Cognitive Development: Tasks for the Teacher 37
Arnold D. Cortazzo

III Border-line Retardation in Low and Middle Income Adolescents 57
David Elkind

IV Cognitive Development— A Means for Maturation and Measurement 87
Robert M. Allen and Barry J. Schwartz

V Psychological Assessment, Developmental Plasticity, and Heredity, With Implications for Early Education 121
J. McV. Hunt

VI Some Applied and Theoretical Implications of Behavior Technology for Mental Retardation 149
Richard P. Toister

Index 157

Foreword

THE SOUTH FLORIDA FOUNDATION for Retarded Children is extremely pleased to sponsor this symposium on the theories dealing with the nature of cognitive growth and development and their implications for the mentally retarded child. The way in which the retarded master and utilize knowledge in appropriate settings is certainly an important concern for the foundation and for society. Such questions as how and when the retarded become ready to learn, the manner and sequence in which they master skills, the approaches in learning that work best for them, and the extent and rate of growth that they can achieve are critical topics for all of us.

The participants in this symposium were selected because of their outstanding contributions in the field of cognitive growth and learning. We are indeed fortunate to have such leaders appearing together, and we take pride in making this research available to the public and to the professional world. We trust that these informative presentations will stimulate further research in the area of cognitive development.

The proceedings of this symposium have raised many definable problems for research. The answers to these questions will be of great benefit to the retarded and a valuable contribution to the whole of humanity.

H. BARNUM SEELEY
President, South Florida Foundation for Retarded Children

Preface

THE PERPLEXING QUESTIONS of how persons who are retarded learn and what can be done to accelerate and augment their learning have been of concern to educators, psychologists, physicians, and parents for centuries. Itard's historic efforts to educate Victor, the Wild Boy of Aveyron, in 1799 inspired many to search for an answer to the enigma. The field of mental retardation credits Itard with developing the first scientific approach to teaching the retarded. Itard had embraced the notion that the final intellectual level that any individual might reach was due largely to environmental forces. In 1866 Sequin in his book *Idiocy: Its Treatment by the Physiological Method* explained retardation on the basis of neurophysiological defects, which, he felt, prevented sensations from reaching the brain. His approach was to make the retarded as efficient as possible through muscle training and physical education. He believed this would increase the efficiency of the transmission of sensations. He further believed that if the sense receptors were bombarded with very strong stimuli and these stimuli were repeated often enough a sufficient number of them would get past the defective parts and to the brain to form adequate associations and learning.

Maria Montessori developed autoeducation procedures in

her efforts to teach the retarded. She felt that a person achieves a level of intellect closely related to the stimuli provided in his environment as a child. Montessori methods have been quite useful with bright and gifted children as well as with the retarded.

Since these first efforts, numerous different physiological, psychological, sociological, and educational procedures, all searching for answers, have been tried with the retarded. This symposium is a still further effort to give the field a better understanding of how the retarded learn. We will never completely conquer this problem unless we in the field consider the important areas of cognitive growth and development. This book, by examining some of the theories of cognitive development with implications for the retarded, brings us another step closer in our search for answers.

JACK W. MCALLISTER
Director, Division of Retardation
Florida Department of Health and Rehabilitative Services

Theories of Cognitive Development

Edward Zigler

Why Retarded Children Do Not Perform Up to the Level of Their Ability

NUMEROUS STUDIES have reported that though matched with normal children on those cognitive measures which constitute mental age, retarded children nevertheless perform inadequately on a variety of problem-solving tasks. Given that the mental age (MA) measure has proven to be a rather effective and far-ranging predictor of intellectual performance, we are faced with the intriguing question of why retarded children behave less adequately on a number of tasks than their MAs would indicate. Two broad, but nevertheless circumscribed, theoretical efforts have been mounted to explain the empirically observed disparity between the retarded child's MA indicator and his performance on tasks not included in IQ assessment. (It should be noted at the outset that the two efforts are not mutually exclusive.)

The more popular of these two explanatory efforts emphasizes cognitive factors, and I refer to it in my writings as the difference orientation. (See Zigler, 1966, 1967, 1969, and 1970 for a complete discussion of the difference orientation.) Difference theorists argue that IQ (on which groups of normal and retarded children still vary even though

Edward Zigler, Ph.D., is professor and director, Child Development Program, Department of Psychology, Yale University.

matched on MA) reflects certain features of physiological and cognitive functioning of the individual, which in turn affect performance on a wide variety of tasks, over and above that difference accounted for by general cognitive level attained. Thus, over the years we have been informed that the retarded suffer from a relative impermeability of the boundaries between regions in the cognitive structure (Kounin, 1941a, 1941b; Lewin, 1936), primary and secondary rigidity caused by subcortical and cortical malformations, respectively (Goldstein, 1942-1943), inadequate neural satiation related to brain modifiability or cortical conductivity (Spitz, 1963), impaired attention-directing mechanisms (Zeaman & House, 1963), a relative brevity in the persistence of stimulus traces (Siegel & Foshee, 1960), and improper development of the verbal system resulting in a dissociation between the verbal and motor systems (Luria, 1956; O'Connor & Hermelin, 1959). Such factors are thought by difference theorists to be inherent in mental retardation (ultimately defined by IQ) and are increasingly used to explain differences in performance between groups of retarded and normal children who, though equated on MA, do indeed continue to differ on IQ.

In opposition to this cognitive difference interpretation, my colleagues and I have championed an explanation of performance differences between MA-matched groups of normal and retarded individuals in terms that highlight the motivational and emotional differences between typical groups of these children. (See Zigler, in press, for a full discussion of the motivational orientation.) Unlike the cognitive factors emphasized by the cognitive difference theorists, the motivational factors emphasized by the motivational theorists are not viewed as inherent in mental retardation per se. Rather, the motivational theorists argue that retarded children are more likely to have a higher incidence of certain experiences in their socialization histories than are normal children. These experiences then are viewed as giving rise to a motivational structure that interferes with optimal performance by the retarded. From this point of view, the child's performance on any task is not seen as the inexorable reflection of the child's cognitive system, but rather as a reflection of at least both this system and the child's motives, attitudes, goals, and general psychological stance toward problems and toward human purveyors of problems. Stated most simply, my view is that retarded children could behave at least as well as would be predicted from their MAs if particular motivational factors did not interfere with and thus attenuate their performance.

Over the years my colleagues and I have attempted to delineate and, on occasion, experimentally manipulate such motivational variables. These factors are not unique to the performance of the retarded, but are particularly relevant to their behavior inasmuch as retarded children as a group tend to encounter certain events much more than do children of normal intellect. We have been interested in discovering the particular experiences that lead to particular motives, attitudes, and styles of the retarded and in discovering how variation in these experiences leads to variation in the personality structure of individuals of both retarded and normal intellect. We have, in certain instances, been especially interested in demonstrating that the performance of a retarded child, which has heretofore been attributed to his cognitive shortcomings, is actually the product of a particular motive. This interest does not mean that we have invariably stressed the importance of motivational over cognitive variables, since clearly these two classes of variables can independently, and in interaction, influence performance on any given task.

Space in this volume does not permit a comprehensive review of the fifteen years of work conducted by my colleagues and myself. This work has been reviewed several times and is easily available. We have demonstrated that much of the behavioral inadequacy of the retarded stems from motives that can be isolated. We have also been successful in demonstrating that the genesis of these motives lies in the socialization histories of retarded individuals rather than in intellectual retardation per se.

Only through a fine-grained analysis of performance on a variety of tasks by a number of groups of retarded and normal subjects with varying socialization histories have we been able to attribute particular aspects of performance to either cognitive or motivational factors. We have also been aware that although it is conceptually feasible to distinguish between cognitive and motivational factors in respect to certain behaviors, this division becomes extremely difficult, if not totally artificial. In much of our work, however, each of these two factors has been sufficiently delineated for us to demonstrate how each, independently, may affect the child's performance.

This discussion is limited to a single but pervasive factor that influences the performance of the retarded, a factor that often causes the retarded to appear less cognitively adequate than they are in fact. The factor to which I am referring is an approach to problem solving characterized by an atypically high degree of outer-directedness as opposed to a willingness to employ one's own cognitive resources, even in those instances in which one's cognitive resources are adequate for successful problem solution. To give my theory away somewhat, this outer-directedness would appear to be the product of the inordinate amount of failure experienced by so many of the retarded when they do attempt to use their cognitive abilities.

I am discussing the outer-directedness phenomenon primarily because it is a phenomenon that partakes of both motivational and cognitive attributes. In my own thinking this factor is situated in that gray area where the variables of motivational and cognitive phenomenon shade each other. My hope, of course, is that by the thorough exploration of such a factor we might further illuminate what are two somewhat artificially constructed types of variables that finally interact to produce the psychodynamic wholeness or complex unity characterizing so much of ongoing human behavior. In other words, although for purposes of analysis it makes sense to divide the person into a set of subsystems, any final theoretical product must restore the oneness of the human being and deal explicitly with the intricacies of the interactions between the subsystems in our theoretical edifice.

As noted, our work now indicates that the high incidence of failure experienced by the retarded generates a style of problem solving characterized by outer-directedness. That is, the retarded child comes to distrust his own solutions to problems and therefore seeks guides for action from the immediate environment. In an early study (Zigler, Hodgden, & Stevenson, 1958) we found that the institutionalized retarded tended to terminate their performance on experimental games when an adult experimenter suggested that they might do so. Normal children tended to ignore such suggestions, stopping instead of their own volition. Originally this finding was discussed in terms of social deprivation and heightened motivation for social reinforcement and was interpreted as reflecting a greater compliance on the part of the institutionalized retarded. The position we then advanced was that social deprivation resulted in an enhanced motivation for social reinforcers and, hence, greater compliance in an effort to obtain such reinforcement. (I think we see here a clear instance of how a commitment to a particular viewpoint leads one to avoid interpretations of data other than the one to which he is committed.)

C. Green and I (1962), however, found that although normal children exhibited little tendency to do so, a higher percentage of noninstitutionalized than institutionalized retarded terminated their performance upon a cue from the experimenter. This finding is incongruent with the social deprivation interpretation, which would predict that the noninstitutionalized retarded would be similar to normal children in their sensitivity to adult cues. This dissimilarity in the performance of the noninstitutionalized retarded and normals led us to suggest that such sensitivity to external cues is most appropriately viewed as a general component of problem solving, having its antecedents in the child's history of success or failure.

Of the three types of children Green and I observed, the normal child would be expected to have had the highest incidence of success emanating from self-initiated solutions to problems. Such a child therefore would be the most willing to use his own thought processes and the solutions they provide in problem-solving situations. Antithetically, the self-initiated solutions of the retarded would be expected to result in a high incidence of failure, thus making the retarded wary of the solutions provided by their own thought processes. This type of child should then evidence a greater sensitivity to external or environmental cues, particularly those provided by social agents, in the belief that these cues would be more reliable indicators than those provided by his own cognitive efforts. Thus the retarded, in general, would be more sensitive to external cues than would normal children. The institutionalized retarded live in an environment adjusted to their intellectual shortcomings and should therefore experience less failure than the noninstitutionalized retarded. This latter type of child must continue to face the complexities and demands of an environment with which he is ill-equipped to deal and, as we found, should manifest the greatest sensitivity to external cues.

This general position was first tested by J. E. Turnure and myself (1964). In a first experiment we examined the imitation behavior of normal and noninstitutionalized retarded children of the same MA on two tasks. One task involved imitating an adult and the other imitating a peer. Prior to the imitation tasks the children played three games under either a success or a failure condition. The specific hypotheses tested were that retarded children would be generally more imitative than normals and that all children would be more imitative following failure experiences than following success experiences. These hypotheses were confirmed on both imitation tasks. To the extent that the behavior of normal children is considered the preferred mode, this study indicated that the outer-directedness of the retarded child results in behavior characterized by an oversensitivity to external models with a resulting lack of spontaneity and creativity. We must emphasize, however, that heightened outer-directedness is not invariably detrimental to performance on problem-solving tasks.

Turnure and I (1964) conducted a second experiment to test further the hypothesis that retarded children are more outer-directed than normal children of the same MA. In this study we tried to demonstrate that outer-directedness may be either detrimental or beneficial, depending upon the nature of the situation. Normal children and noninstitutionalized retarded children of the same MA were instructed to assemble an item, reminiscent of the object-assembly items on the WISC, as quickly as they could. While the subject assembled the item, the adult experimenter put together a second object-assembly item. The hypothesis was that the outer-directedness of the retarded child would lead him to attend to what the experimenter was doing rather than to concentrate on his own task and thus interfere with his performance. When the child had completed his puzzle, the experimenter took apart the puzzle that he himself had been working on. He then gave this second puzzle to the child and told him to put it together as quickly as he could. Here the cues that the retarded child had picked up as a result of his outer-directedness should facilitate performance on the second puzzle. The predictions were again confirmed. The normal children were superior to the retarded on the first task, whereas the retarded were superior to the normal children on the second task. No statistically significant differences were found in a control condition in which the experimenter did not put together the second object-assembly task while the subject was working on the first. Further confirmation of the outer-directedness hypothesis was obtained by a direct measure of the frequency with which the children actually glanced at the experimenter. As expected the retarded subjects glanced at the experimenter significantly more often than the normal children.

The findings of this study not only confirmed the hypothesis that retarded children are more outer-directed in their problem solving, but also suggested the process by which the outer-directed style of the retarded is reinforced and perpetuated. Undoubtedly the child is rewarded for careful attentiveness to adults in many real-life situations. In many situations such attending clearly will be detrimental to the child's problem solving. Across tasks, optimal problem solving requires a child to utilize both external cues and his own cognitive resources. The retarded child's overreliance on external cues is understandable in view of his life history. The intermittent success accruing to the retarded child as a result of such a style, in combination with his generally lowered expectation of success (see Zigler, in press) across problem-solving situations, suggests the great utility that such outer-directedness would have for the retarded.

A further test of the hypothesis that retarded are more outer-directed than normal children was conducted by B. Sanders, E. C. Butterfield, and myself (Sanders, Zigler, & Butterfield, 1968). The central question we addressed was whether the outer-directedness of the retarded, found on simple imitation and object-assembly tasks, also manifests itself in a standard discrimination learning situation. The discovery that the retarded child's outer-directedness influences even his performance on a discrimination learning task would indicate that this style of problem solving is a relatively pervasive one which should be considered when evaluating the general behavior of the retarded. Groups of normal and retarded children of the same MA were compared on a size discrimination task involving the presentation of an additional cue that the subject could use in choosing between stimuli. Three conditions were used: (a) one in which the subject's response to the cue would lead to success (positive condition), (b) one in which it would lead to failure (negative condition), and (c) one in which no cue was presented (control condition). The expectation was that the cue would be more enhancing in the positive and more debilitating in the negative condition to the performance of the retarded than to the performance of the normal children. Although some rather complex findings obtained in the positive condition lent some weight to the outer-directedness hypothesis, this hypothesis received its strongest support under the negative condition. The retarded made significantly more errors than normals in the negative condition. Furthermore, the retarded made significantly more cued than noncued errors, whereas there was no difference between cued and noncued errors for normals. Thus the retarded relied heavily upon the negative cue, even though it led to errors, and the normals did not. This study provides additional evidence of an outer-directed style of problem solving in retarded individuals.

Further work on the outer-directedness hypothesis was conducted in a series of three experiments by Thomas Achenbach and myself (1968) in which this hypothesis was reformulated in terms of a distinction between two contrasting learning strategies, defined by the degree of reliance upon situational cues as guides to behavior. Achenbach and I described these two strategies as follows: (a) The cue-learning strategy was defined as problem-solving behavior characterized by a reliance on concrete situational cues such that overt behavior is guided by the cues with little attempt being made to educe relations among problem elements. (b) The contrasting problem-learning strategy was defined as problem-solving behavior characterized by active attempts to educe abstract relations among problem elements in order to proceed from these relations to the solution of the problem. This distinction is reminiscent of E. C. Tolman's (1948) distinction between "narrow strip" and "broad comprehensive" cognitive maps and J. S. Bruner's (1965) distinction between "extrinsic" and "intrinsic" problem solving.

Although our procedure varied somewhat across the three experiments, essentially we utilized a three-choice size discrimination task in which a light came on in association with the correct stimulus. On the first few trials of this learning task, the light came on almost immediately. As the trials progressed, however, the interval between the onsets of the trial and of the light became longer and longer. Throughout the trials the subject was occasionally prodded to choose his stimulus as quickly as possible. This procedure was intended to create a somewhat ambiguous situation in which the child could either continue waiting for the light to direct his choice or begin responding to the abstract relation (relative size) among the problem elements. Correct responses before the light onset were the measure of successful use of the problem-learning strategy. Control groups were also used in which groups of subjects learned the discrimination without a light cue.

In our first experiment we examined the performance of institutionalized retarded, noninstitutionalized retarded, and normal children matched for MA. (As noted previously, the noninstitutionalized retarded should be even more reliant on external cues than should the institutionalized retarded because the environment of the latter, which is geared more to their abilities, reduces the failure experiences leading to reliance on external cues.) In the control condition the learning performances of the three groups were quite comparable. As predicted, however, in the cue condition the retarded relied on the cue significantly longer than the normals. Furthermore, the noninstitutionalized retarded relied on the cue significantly longer than the institutionalized retarded.

In a second experiment groups of normals and noninstitutionalized retarded were presented the learning tasks immediately after experiencing either success or failure. In this experiment some further control groups were established to allow us to assess whether waiting for the light cue inhibited learning of the size relation or was just a conservative response strategy whereby the subject decided to wait for the light even though he knew that size determined the correct stimulus. In this experiment we replicated the findings of our first experiment and also demonstrated that reliance on the cue by the retarded involved an inhibition of learning rather than caution in responding. Contrary to our expectations, our failure and success manipulations did not significantly influence the reliance on cues either by the normals or by the retarded.

During this study, however, we obtained some rather serendipitous support for our view that the relative incidence of success and failure experienced by the child is what determines his outer-directedness as defined by reliance on cues. We discovered a class of sixteen retarded children whose teacher used teaching methods directed to the long-term manipulation of precisely those variables that we thought mediated outer-directedness. Observation of his classroom made it clear that he showered new pupils with success experiences and attempted to increase their self-esteem. Thereafter, he specifically reinforced what he called "figuring things out for yourself," rewarding independent thought more highly than correct responses. We examined the performance of these sixteen retarded subjects on our learning task and discovered not only that they relied on cues significantly less than our other retarded children but that they relied on them less, albeit not significantly so, than did the children of normal intellect. Again, we see that it is not the retardation per se that produces the behavior but rather the particular experiences to which retarded children are subjected.

In a third experiment Achenbach and I found a significant correlation between imitation of an adult and the number of trials taken to give up reliance on the cue in the learning task by the retarded, but not by normals. This finding suggested that the reliance on external cues constituted a more general, less task-specific strategy for the retarded than for the normal child. The findings of a later study by Achenbach (1969), however, indicated that for normal children the cue-learning strategy is not necessarily task-specific, since such cue dependency was found to be related to the normal child's impulsivity as well as to the higher intellectual processes involved in analogical reasoning. It thus appears that for normals and the retarded reliance on cues in a discrimination learning problem is but one manifestation of a general style of problem solving.

What must be noted at this point is that the retarded child is not more outer-directed than the normal child simply because he has a lower IQ. How outer-directed any child will be depends on two factors: the level of cognition attained, e.g., MA, and the degree of success experienced by using his cognitive resources. Ignoring the second factor, we may assert that the lower the MA, the more outer-directed the child, because such outer-directedness would be more conducive to successful problem solving than dependence upon poorly developed cognitive abilities. With the growth and development of greater cognitive resources the child should become more inner-directed, because such cognitive development reduces the child's dependence on external cues. Furthermore, independence training with increasing age is characterized by a continuous reduction in the cues provided the child by adults, which further reduces the effectiveness of an outer-directed style. Thus, the shift from outer- to inner-directedness in normal development is a product of both the increasing cognitive ability of the child and the withdrawal of external cues that had previously made the outer-directed style effective.

This argument involving the level of cognition factor does not explain the findings previously reported which indicated that the retarded are more outer-directed than normal children even when matched on MA. Here the crucial variable would appear not to be the level of cognition attained but rather the particular success to failure history experienced by the child when using his cognitive resources. Apparently society reacts to a child more on the basis of the child's chronological age (CA) than his mental age. Indeed, certain age expectancies are firmly built into our child-training practices. The normal child's mental age is commensurate with his CA, and he is continuously presented problems that are in keeping with his cognitive resources. With increasing maturity he experiences more and more success in utilizing these resources in dealing with problems. The retarded child, on the other hand, is continuously confronted with problems appropriate to his CA but inappropriate to his MA. These problems are simply too difficult for him, and he does not experience the degree of success that would lead him to discard his outer-directedness in favor of reliance on his own cognitive abilities.

The most comprehensive investigation of the outer-directedness phenomenon done to date was conducted by Regina Yando and myself (1971). We felt that although the studies just reported generally supported the outer-directedness formulation, there were also some inconsistent findings across the studies, as well as some findings not in keeping with the views that have been advanced concerning the genesis of this style of problem solving. For instance, whereas in two of the studies (Achenbach & Zigler, 1968; Turnure & Zigler, 1964) we found differences in outer-directedness between groups of normal and familial retarded, in another study (Sanders, Zigler, & Butterfield, 1968) we found differences between groups of normals and organic retarded, but not between groups of normals and familial retarded. To account for this finding, Sanders, Butterfield, and I offered a post hoc explanation involving differences in parental expectancies of intellectual success.

We asserted that an important determinant of outer-directedness was the degree to which a child's intellectual performance meets parental expectations. Noting that the organic retarded come from homes with higher intellectual expectations than those of the familial retarded, we concluded that these expectations result in phenomenologically more failure in the organic than in the familial retarded and, thus, lead to greater outer-directedness in the organic group. However, another explanation can be advanced. Since we did not use etiology as a dimension in our design, our groups of organic and familial retarded were not equated on MA and IQ. Our finding could thus be the result of comparing lower IQ and lower MA organic children and higher IQ and higher MA familial children with a group of normal children whose MA fell between the two groups of retarded children. Selecting one explanation over the other requires a design involving a comparison of groups of organic and familial retarded equated on both MA and IQ with a group of normal children of the same MA.

Another aspect of the outer-directedness formulation that was in need of further illumination was the concept that, independent of IQ, younger children would be more outer-directed than older children. The one study (Achenbach & Zigler, 1968) in which we attempted to test the general developmental aspect of the outer-directedness formulation resulted in failure to verify a major tenet of this position, namely, that there should be less dependence on external cues at higher than at lower cognitive levels.

In our study of outer-directedness R. Yando and I compared the performance of eight groups of children (institutionalized and noninstitutionalized organic retarded, familial retarded, normal children matched to the retarded groups on MA, and normal children matched to the retarded groups on CA) on discrimination learning and imitation tasks. The discrimination learning task, also used by Sanders et al. (1968), involved a cue that, if followed, would result in poorer learning. The other measure of outer-directedness was an imitation task similar to the one used by Turnure and myself (1964), which involved imitating a design. The focus of this study was primarily on the effects of etiology of retardation and institutionalization on the degree of outer-directedness manifested. Because we used both MA and CA controls for the two retarded groups, we had two groups of normal children at different cognitive levels, so we could further test the proposition that outer-directedness decreases with increasing cognitive capacity.

The hypothesis that retarded children are more outer-directed than normal children received further support in this study. On the discrimination learning task, the retarded children made significantly more cued than noncued errors. This reliance on situational cues was particularly striking because both of the normal groups made significantly fewer cued than noncued errors. Given the nature of the task, the tendency over trials should be to make fewer cued than noncued errors because the light becomes a discriminable cue associated with nonreinforcement. Retarded subjects nevertheless persisted in selecting the cued stimulus even though their responses were not reinforced. The question may be raised whether this self-defeating behavior is a result of the retarded child's outer-directedness manifesting itself in a strategy that does not permit the child to resist the cue, or is better understood in terms of an IQ-associated inability to learn the size discrimination. That it is a strategy phenomenon rather than a result of an inherent inability to learn was suggested by the ability of the retarded to learn as well as the normals in the control condition where no cue was present. On the imitation task, as with the discrimination learning findings, the retarded children were more imitative than the normals.

Support for the general developmental aspect of the outer-directedness formulation was found in the imitation data. The younger normal children imitated significantly more than did the older normal children. The failure to find differences between the two age groups for the cued versus noncued error data of the discrimination learning task may have been because the task was perceived as equally easy by both groups. That it was in fact equally easy for both CA levels is indicated by the similarity of the performance of both groups in the control condition. A major tenet of the outer-directedness position is that, across all persons, outer-directedness will increase as a task becomes more difficult and ambiguous. It thus appears that although not terribly difficult the imitation task introduced enough ambiguity for age differences in outer-directedness to become manifest whereas the discrimination learning task did not.

The Yando and Zigler study produced a number of findings associated with the factor of institutionalization of both normal and retarded children and with the role of etiology of retardation. These findings should be noted since they appear capable of clarifying further the dynamics of outer-directedness. Although not found in retarded children, the pattern of making more noncued than cued errors was more marked for the institutionalized than the noninstitutionalized normal children. It is interesting that, in the experimental condition of the discrimination learning task, the institutionalized normals often verbalized their feelings that the experimenter was "trying to fool me." The life experiences of institutionalized normal children apparently precipitate suspiciousness and wariness, which result in these children learning very quickly to actively avoid an erroneous cue provided by an adult. My associates and I (cf. Zigler, in press) have presented considerable evidence that early negative experiences at the hands of adults result in just such wariness or suspiciousness, a characteristic that we have labeled the negative reaction tendency. This tendency has been found to be especially related to the factors of the nature of the relationship between the child's parents and the parents' mental health. It is therefore of some interest to note that of the forty-eight institutionalized normal children used for the Yando and Zigler study, twenty had at least one parent who had been diagnosed as mentally ill, seventeen had come from broken homes, and sixteen had been classified as neglected. The finding that the institutionalized younger normals imitated less than the noninstitutionalized normals may be a further reflection of such a negative reaction tendency.

Explaining the tendency of institutionalized normal children to make relatively few cued as compared to noncued errors in terms of their early social deprivation raises an interesting question. Why is the same tendency not found in the institutionalized familial retarded who also tend to be institutionalized following rather severe early social deprivation? The crucial factor here appears to be the IQ of the child. If the child's intellect is adequate, he can choose to use or not to use the cues provided by an adult. If his past interactions with adults have been negative, it is reasonable that he will opt to avoid adults and the cues they provide. The child with a lower intellectual capacity does not enjoy such freedom of choice. Regardless of his personal attitudes toward adults, his own failure experiences when confronted with problems have taught him that it is better to use the cues provided by a possibly punishing adult than to rely on his own cognitive resources. Such an interpretation is bolstered by the findings (Irons & Zigler, 1969; Zigler, 1961; Zigler, Balla, & Butterfield, 1968) of a negative relation between preinstitutional social deprivation and the effectiveness of social reinforcers dispensed by an adult for institutionalized children of normal intellect and of a positive relation for institutionalized retarded children.

In the Yando and Zigler study institutionalization was also found to affect differentially the outer-directedness of the two groups of retarded children. The noninstitutionalized organics' performance on the learning task was significantly more outer-directed than that of the institutionalized organics whereas the performance of the noninstitutionalized familials was less outer-directed than the institutionalized familials. These findings lend some credence to the suggestion of Sanders et al. (1968) that the noninstitutionalized organically retarded child who remains in the home faces greater expectations and, consequently, more failure (often exacerbated by the achievement of siblings), resulting in more outer-directedness than he would face if he lived in an institutional environment adjusted to his intellectual shortcomings. That the less failure-ridden institutional environment decreases the outer-directedness of the organics was further underlined by the Yando and Zigler finding that the longer the organic retarded child was institutionalized, the less outer-directed he was.

The performance of the institutionalized and noninstitutionalized organics supports Turnure and Zigler's (1964) suggestion that the distractibility so frequently attributed to the retarded, rather than being an inherent characteristic, may, in part, reflect their outer-directedness. If attending to the light cue is viewed as a form of distractibility, then the lesser distractibility in the institutionalized as compared to the noninstitutionalized organics and the decrease in distractibility with increasing institutionalization mean that this sort of distractibility reflects a style of problem solving rather than a reaction stemming inextricably from the organicity itself.

The finding that the noninstitutionalized familials were (at a border-line level of significance) less outer-directed than institutionalized familials is in opposition to the findings of Achenbach and Zigler (1968). This variance in findings may be because the institutionalized familials in the Achenbach and Zigler study were older than the noninstitutionalized familials, and both the institutionalized and noninstitutionalized familial groups in the Achenbach and Zigler study were older than the familials used in Yando and Zigler. It should also be noted that Achenbach and Zigler used a procedure in which responding to the cue resulted in a correct response, whereas in the present study the cue resulted in an incorrect response. Furthermore, comparing studies involving different institutions as well as interpreting the institutional effects discovered in the present study demand considerable caution. Considerable evidence (reviewed by Zigler, in press) has now been presented which indicates that the effects of institutionalization on a child vary both as a function of the particular nature of the institution and the particular preinstitutional history of the child.

The findings of the Yando and Zigler study in conjunction with earlier findings underline the value of the outer-directedness concept for the understanding of children's problem solving. These findings certainly support my general argument, which calls into question the practice of viewing the performance of all children, and especially the retarded, on problem-solving tasks as the reflection of cognitive abilities alone. The outer-directedness findings reported here may be used in explaining the great suggestibility so frequently attributed to the retarded child (e.g., Davies, 1959). Studies by J. V. Hottel (1960) and L. J. Lucito (1959), which demonstrated that duller pupils showed more frequent conformity to group decisions than did brighter subjects under ambiguous stimulus conditions where the group made the wrong decision, are in keeping with our views concerning outer-directedness. Lucito's interpretation of these findings was that, as a result of their previous experiences, the brighter children saw themselves as successful in interpreting objective reality and as definers of social reality for others. The duller children, however, more frequently failed at interpreting objective reality and therefore looked to others to define social reality for them.

Also consistent with other studies are our findings that it is the noninstitutionalized retarded child who must continually meet the expectancies of a world with which he is ill-equipped to deal, and who is therefore more outer-directed than the institutionalized retarded child who resides in a less demanding environment more geared to his intellectual shortcomings. Our findings are in keeping with those of M. Rosen, J. C. Diggory, and B. Werlinsky (1966) that indicate that residential care is more likely to foster the retarded child's optimism and self-confidence than is the nonsheltered school in the community setting. These investigators found that, compared to the noninstitutionalized retarded, the institutionalized retarded set higher goals, predicted better performance for themselves, and actually performed at a higher level. R. B. Edgerton and G. Sabagh (1962) also pointed out certain positive features of the sheltered institutional setting for the high-level retarded child. They note certain "aggrandizements" of the self that are available, such as the presence of inferior low-level retarded children with whom they can compare themselves favorably, their far greater social success within the institution, and mutual support for face-saving rationales concerning their presence there. This argument is similar to that presented by G. O. Johnson and S. A. Kirk (1950), who favor separate special classes for retarded children in public schools because these children tend to be isolated and rejected in regular classes.

As noted previously, the outer-directedness formulation may also be relevant to the distractibility of the retarded. We may hypothesize that outer-directedness, which is learned relatively early owing to the rather effective cues provided by adults and peers, would generalize to a multiplicity of other external stimuli. This generalization would impel the child to attend to a wide variety of stimuli impinging upon him, since such behavior has been conducive to more successful problem solving. Such a style should be given up relatively early in the development of the normal child, but should continue to be characteristic of the retarded child because of the inordinate amount of failure he experiences when relying on his own resources. One would probably describe a child who utilizes such a style as being distractible, and, in fact, distractibility has often been attributed to the retarded child (Cruse, 1961; Goldstein & Seigel, 1961). The outer-directedness hypothesis suggests that distractibility, rather than being an inherent characteristic of the retarded, actually reflects a style of problem solving emanating from the particular experiential histories of these children. Some support for such a view was recently presented by Turnure (1970), who examined the glancing behavior of retarded children and found that such glancing was motivated by information-seeking and was not a type of random behavior that one would ascribe to a neurological problem, nor was it some vacuous orientation to salient social stimuli. Assuming that distractibility reflects a particular type of problem solving, one would expect this style of problem solving and the trait of distractibility in normal children whose self-initiated solutions to problems have often been inadequate (e.g., the very young child), or the inappropriately reinforced child (e.g., the child whose parents make intellectual demands not in keeping with the child's cognitive ability).

The research I have reported in this paper involves but one of many factors that we have found to attenuate retarded children's performance below that which would be expected from their cognitive levels. This research has been conducted within a general framework that emphasizes the value of a systematic evaluation of the role of affective, motivational, and personality factors. An understanding of these factors and their relation to intellectual level will provide a better comprehension of why retarded children do not perform up to their level of cognitive ability and how we might help them to do so. Considerable evidence suggests that our efforts to optimize the behavior of the retarded by changing learned motivational patterns would have considerable payoff.

Although the majority of the efforts and environmental manipulation designed to improve the quality of cognitive functioning in the retarded have been relatively unsuccessful (see reviews by Jones, 1954; Zigler, 1966), a growing body of evidence indicates that certain motivational and personality factors relevant to social adjustment are considerably more modifiable. As L. S. Penrose (1963) noted after a lifetime of work with the retarded:

> The most important work carried out in the field of training defectives is unspectacular. It is not highly technical but requires unlimited patience, good will and common sense. The reward is to be expected not so much in scholastic improvement of the patient as in his personal adjustment to social life. Occupations are found for patients of all grades so that they can take part as fully and usefully as possible in human affairs. This process, which has been termed socialization, contributes greatly to the happiness not only of the patients themselves, but also to those who are responsible for their care (p. 282).

It is perhaps within this area of socialization that we can do a great deal to enhance the everyday effectiveness of the retarded. Both B. S. Burks (1939) and A. M. Leahy (1935) discovered that personality and character traits were more influenced by environment than many modifiable factors which are important in the determination of social adjustment. It is not rare to encounter individuals with the same intellectual makeup demonstrating quite disparate social adjustments. Perhaps then the important question concerning the socialization potential of retarded individuals centers less on the problem of how to improve their cognitive functioning than on the question of how we might provide the retarded with those experiences that result in the full utilization of their intellectual resources, whatever their cognitive ability may be.

References

Achenbach, T. Cue-learning, associative responding, and school performance in children. *Developmental Psychology,* 1969, **1**, 717-725.

Achenbach, T., & Zigler, E. Cue-learning and problem-learning strategies in normal and retarded children. *Child Development,* 1968, **39**, 827-848.

Bruner, J. S. The growth of mind. *American Psychologist,* 1965, **20**, 1007-10017.

Burks, B. S. Review of Marie Skodak, *Children in foster homes: A study of mental development. Journal of Educational Psychology,* 1939, **30**, 548-555.

Cruse, D. Effects of distractions upon the performance of brain-injured and familial retarded children. *American Journal of Mental Deficiency,* 1961, **66**, 86-92.

Davies, S. P. *The mentally retarded in society.* New York: Columbia University Press, 1959.

Edgerton, R. B., & Sabagh, G. From mortification to aggrandizement: Changing self-conception in the careers of the mentally retarded. *Psychiatry,* 1962, **25**, 263-272.

Goldstein, H., & Seigel, D. Characteristics of educable mentally handicapped children. In W. Rothstein (Ed.), *Mental retardation: Readings and resources.* New York: Holt, Rinehart & Winston, 1961.

Goldstein, K. Concerning rigidity. *Character and Personality,* 1942-1943, **11**, 209-226.

Green, C., & Zigler, E. Social deprivation and the performance of feebleminded and normal children on a satiation type task. *Child Development,* 1962, 33, 499-508.

Hottel, J. V. The influence of age and intelligence on independence-conformity behavior of children. Unpublished doctoral dissertation, George Peabody College for Teachers, 1960.

Irons, N., & Zigler, E. Children's responsiveness to social reinforcement as a function of short-term preliminary social interactions and long-term social deprivation. *Developmental Psychology,* 1969, 1, 402-409.

Johnson, G. O., & Kirk, S. A. Are mentally handicapped children segregated in the regular grades? *Exceptional Children,* 1950, 17, 65-68.

Jones, H. E. The environment and mental development. In L. Carmichael (Ed.), *Manual of child psychology.* (2nd ed.) New York: Wiley, 1954.

Kounin, J. Experimental studies of rigidity: I. The measurement of rigidity in normal and feebleminded persons. *Character and Personality,* 1941, 9, 251-272. (a)

Kounin, J. Experimental studies of rigidity: II. The explanatory power of the concept of rigidity as applied to feeblemindedness. *Character and Personality,* 1941, 9, 273-282. (b)

Leahy, A. M. Nature-nurture and intelligence. *Genetic Psychology Monographs,* 1935, 17, 236-308.

Lewin, K. *A dynamic theory of personality.* New York: McGraw-Hill, 1936.

Lucito, L. J. A comparison of independence-conformity behavior of intellectually bright and dull children. Unpublished doctoral dissertation, University of Illinois, 1959.

Luria, A. R. *Problems of higher nervous activity in the normal and non-normal child.* Moscow: Akad. Pedag. Nauk RSFSR, 1956.

O'Connor, N., & Hermelin, B. Discrimination and reversal learning in imbeciles. *Journal of Abnormal and Social Psychology,* 1959, 59, 409-413.

Penrose, L. S. *The biology of mental defect.* London: Sidgwick & Jackson, 1963.

Rosen, M., Diggory, J. C., & Werlinsky, B. Goal setting and expectancy of success in institutionalized and noninstitutionalized mental subnormals. *American Journal of Mental Deficiency,* 1966, 71, 249-255.

Sanders, B., Zigler, E., & Butterfield, E. C. Outer-directedness in the discrimination learning of normal and mentally retarded children. *Journal of Abnormal Psychology,* 1968, 73, 368-375.

Siegel, P. S., & Foshee, J. G. Molar variability in the mentally defective. *Journal of Abnormal and Social Psychology,* 1960, 61, 141-143.

Spitz, H. H. Field theory in mental deficiency. In N. R. Ellis (Ed.),

Handbook of mental deficiency. New York: McGraw-Hill, 1963.

Tolman, E. C. Cognitive maps in rats and men. *Psychological Review,* 1948, **55**, 189-208.

Turnure, J. E. Reactions to physical and social distractors by moderately retarded, institutionalized children. *Journal of Special Education,* 1970, 283-294.

Turnure, J. E., & Zigler, E. Outer-directedness in the problem solving of normal and retarded children. *Journal of Abnormal and Social Psychology,* 1964, **69**, 427-436.

Yando, R., & Zigler, E. Outerdirectedness in the problem-solving of institutionalized and noninstitutionalized normal and retarded children. *Developmental Psychology,* 1971, **4**, 277-288.

Zeaman, D., & House, B. J. The role of attention in retardate discrimination learning. In N. R. Ellis (Ed.), *Handbook of mental deficiency.* New York: McGraw-Hill, 1963.

Zigler, E. Social deprivation and rigidity in the performance of feebleminded children. *Journal of Abnormal and Social Psychology,* 1961, **62**, 413-421.

Zigler, E. Mental retardation: Current issues and approaches. In M. L. Hoffman & L. W. Hoffman (Eds.), *Review of child development research.* Vol. 2. New York: Russell Sage, 1966.

Zigler, E. Familial mental retardation: A continuing dilemma. *Science,* 1967, **155**, 292-298.

Zigler, E. Developmental versus difference theories of mental retardation and the problem of motivation. *American Journal of Mental Deficiency,* 1969, **73**, 536-556.

Zigler, E. The nature-nurture issue reconsidered: A discussion of Uzgiris' paper. In H. C. Haywood (Ed.), *Social-cultural aspects of mental retardation.* New York: Appleton-Century-Crofts, 1970.

Zigler, E. The retarded child as a whole person. In H. E. Adams & W. K. Boardman, III (Eds.), *Advances in experimental clinical psychology.* Vol. 1. New York: Pergamon Press, in press.

Zigler, E., Balla, D., & Butterfield, E. C. A longitudinal investigation of the relationship between preinstitutional social deprivation and social motivation in institutionalized retardates. *Journal of Personality and Social Psychology,* 1968, **10**, 437-445.

Zigler, E., Hodgden, L., & Stevenson, H. W. The effect of support on the performance of normal and feebleminded children. *Journal of Personality,* 1958, **26**, 106-122.

Arnold D. Cortazzo

The Transactional Approach in Cognitive Development: Tasks for the Teacher

THE NATURE of cognitive growth as described by J. Bruner (1966) is the way in which individuals increase their mastery in acquiring and in utilizing knowledge. He states that cognitive growth relates to the means by which human beings represent their experiences of the world, how they store, integrate, and organize information for future planning and use. To him cognitive growth is a series of psychological events that require explanation in terms of psychological processes.

At first the child's world is known to him mainly by the habitual actions he uses in his attempts to cope with it. This is called the enactive mode. In time a technique of representation through imagery that is relatively free of actions is added called the ikonic mode. Later a new and a more powerful method of representation, the symbolic mode, gradually evolves when the child translates action and imagery into language. Each of the three modes of representation has its own unique way of representing events. Each makes a powerful impression on the mental development of individuals at different ages. The interplay of the modes

Arnold D. Cortazzo, Ed.D., is Director of Research at the Division of Retardation, Florida Department of Health and Rehabilitative Services, Tallahassee.

continues as one of the basic features of adult intellectual life.

Whether or not growth occurs through various stages or is a gradual process is a fruitless debate, according to Bruner, because the growth curve of an individual is very much a function of the behavior one is observing. But, he adds, that the growth of the individual's cognitive ability necessitates an explanation from both the "outside" and the "inside." The helplessness of the child early in his life, for example, appears to be accompanied by an inner, propelling curiosity about the environment and by great self-reinforcing activity (apparently made to achieve success in that environment).

Whether one calls this curiosity "a will to learn" (Bruner, 1966), intrinsic motivation (Hunt, 1965), or a "competence motive" (White, 1959), it seems to be somewhat dependent on and related to an outside supply of stimulation. Both D. Elkind and E. Zigler stress motivational factors in their papers in this book. Elkind gives considerable attention to motivational aspects and theories. Zigler goes one step farther than Elkind by discussing the outer-directedness phenomenon which he believes partakes of both motivational and cognitive attributes. In his thinking this factor is located in the "gray area" where the motivational and cognitive variables shade each other. He believes that a thorough exploration of the outer-directedness factor might make clearer the two artificially constructed types of variables that interact in producing the psychodynamic wholeness of human behavior.

Jean Piaget, one of the early pioneers in the study of cognitive development, characterizes intelligence as an adaptive process in which the environment continuously forces the individual to adapt himself to the reality situation and in turn the individual constantly modifies the environment by imposing on it a structure of its own. Piaget's approach is developmental in nature. He insists that we cannot determine where intelligence starts, "but we can plot its course of development and its ultimate goal." The variable structures—motor or intellectual on the one hand and affective on the other—are the organizational forms of mental ability.

They too are organized along two dimensions: intrapersonal and social or interpersonal (Robinson, 1965).

Piaget views mental development from the child to the adolescent as continuous construction that becomes more solid with each addition. However, there is a distinction between the variable structures that define the successive states of equilibrium[1] and a certain constant functioning that assures the transition from any one state to another. For greater clarity, Piaget distinguishes six stages or periods of development that mark the appearances of these successively constructed structures (Piaget, 1967):

1. The stage at which the first instinctual reflexes, e.g., the grasping reflex, the moro reflex, and the sucking reflex, are simply practiced and the nutritional drives and the first emotions also appear.

2. The stage where the first motor habits, the first organized precepts, and the first differentiated emotions appear.

3. The stage of sensorimotor intelligence (prior to language), of rudimentary affective organization, and of initial affective fixations. The first three stages constitute the infancy period (from birth until the age of one and one-half to two years).

4. The stage of intuitive intelligence, or spontaneous interpersonal feelings, and of social relations in which the child is subordinate to the adult (ages two to seven years, or "early childhood").

5. The stage of organization of concrete intellectual operations (the beginnings of logic) and of moral and social feel-

1. Piaget defines adaptation as the state in which assimilation and accommodation are in equilibrium, which amounts, he says, to saying that an equilibrium exists in the interaction between the environment and the organism. Piaget believes that every mental act can be analyzed according to the balance that exists between assimilation and accommodation.

ings of sharing and cooperation (ages seven to eleven or twelve, or "middle childhood").

6. The stage of formal abstract intellectual operations, of the development of the personality, and of emotional and intellectual entry into the society of adults (the period of adolescence to adulthood).

Each stage is characterized by the new, original structures that distinguish it from previous stages. The basics of the successive constructions are present at the next stages in the form of substructures onto which new characteristics have been added. It follows then in the grown human being that each stage he has gone through corresponds to a given level in the overall hierarchy of behavior. However, temporary and secondary characteristic structures are also at each stage. Thus mental growth is effectuated in the direction of an ever-increasing equilibrium.

Most theories of intelligence, although developmental, have presented a picture of a mind that remains qualitatively stable as it slowly produces knowledge over the childhood years, "a mind which changes in size, but not in shape, so to speak" (Flavell, 1963, p. 381). If the human mind is likened to a computer, this is tantamount to saying that the essential data-processing characteristics of the mind remain invariant from birth onward and that changes occur primarily in the storage or memory units (Robinson, 1965).

Piaget has given us a picture where the individual, as a result of interrelating with the environment during his formative years, constantly forms variable structures or different levels of integration. These structures are both quantitatively and qualitatively different from the syntheses out of which they evolved. He thus sees the human mind as a computer that changes its data-processing characteristics as well as the amount of data it retains in its memory units.

Piaget's approach forces us to look at the retarded for what they are—human beings with a positive potential—rather than for what they are not—defective beings with negative labels. What emerges then is a fuller picture of any child who is retarded at a certain level of development as in transit from one whole way of thinking to another. The mind is seen as a dynamic system, which en route to maturity passes through qualitatively different levels of integration. The traditional view attributed a child's mental ability largely to genetic factors and held that the child's inborn or latent traits would gradually display themselves through the maturation process. However, in all fairness to the thinking at that time, the feeling was that training could help influence the expressions of these traits. This view was a fairly static appraisal of the child, especially of the retarded person.

Such views about the child are still fairly widespread today among teachers, physicians, parents, and the public at large. Intelligence to many is seen as unchanging and somewhat rigid, or a good deal fixed and static. It is thought to be established completely early in life through genetic endowment, and it unfolds according to a genetic blueprint.

Development was thought also to be pretty well predetermined. Further, if potential was seen as innate and cultures were also assumed to be fairly well fixed or constant or very slow changing, then the tasks of the school and the teacher were clear: the teacher was to teach the child according to his fixed potential. If the child did not learn, it was because of the child's genetic makeup, lack of ability, lack of maturation, or lack of physiological and educational readiness. For the child to learn he must be on the appropriate level in terms of maturation, readiness for the task, and interest. The learner was seen this way by most of us not too many years ago (Gordon, 1966), and these views are still held today by many people in the field of mental retardation.

We also believed that experience during the early years, especially prior to the development of speech, was unimportant, because, if intelligence was already predetermined and established, then early experience had little to do with it. The predetermined unfolding maturational process seemed to be all important and inclusive (B. Gardner, 1971).

We felt learning had to be motivated by a homeostatic need or by painful stimulation or by some acquired drives based upon need or stimulation. In other words, for the child to learn he had to be rewarded for the correct response and punished for the wrong response. The child himself had to have the drive to attain personal satisfaction. If he did, then he would give us the right response, the one that we sought. This basic principle is contained in the philosophy of the old adage, "Spare the rod; spoil the child." If you punished the child enough when he was doing something wrong, he would soon stop doing what was wrong. Inherent in this belief was the concept that this method is what discipline is all about, because of the nature of mental organization on the part of the child.

We also thought that intelligence was more or less a monolithic quality. When individual differences in children were discussed, the implication was that children had more of, or less of, the same quality. All intelligence was under one label of IQ, either above average, normal, low, or severely low. The underlying implication of this assumption was that if the child had a lot of intelligence or a high IQ then fine, we could predict great things for him. On the other hand, if he had less intelligence, we would certainly understand by not predicting great things for him. Rather, we would accept his low intelligence and at the same time we would be patient with him.

The notion of a monolithic quality has presented us with some real problems in education, especially in the placement of children in appropriate educational programs. For example, if some children were found to have less than border-line intelligence when compared with other children, they were placed in a special kind of class. If the children were found to have more than average intelligence, they were placed in another kind of special class so that they could have different kinds of experiences. Obviously, both these groups will be reinforced for different sets or kinds of learning and behavior than the children placed in normal or average IQ classes. Yet, if we were to study closely those in the classes for the lower intelligence group, we would find a variety of individual differences among the children even with the same identical low IQ score. We could expect that these variations would also hold true for the children in the higher IQ group with the same identical high IQ scores. Close examination of the educational, social, and psychological needs of the children in both the higher and the lower IQ classes would most likely reveal that they could derive greater educational benefits by being placed with normal IQ classes for certain kinds of programs or activities.

The new concept of intellectual development and functioning has made us keenly sensitive to and aware of the qualitative differences among children with the same identical IQ, differences that cannot and must not be handled by the IQ label alone (B. Gardner, 1971). In fact, it is strongly possible that because of motivation and creativity, individuals with IQs in the 100 range will achieve higher academic status than individuals in the 125 IQ range. Furthermore, some persons in the 80 IQ range who are motivated quite possibly would outachieve persons who are unmotivated in the normal IQ range. Let me add, of course, that these comparisons are hypothetically projected on children of the same ages.

What we have said about motivation and achievement and individual variations in the different groups also applies to creativity and special talents among the individuals in all three groups. Creativity and special talents need not be restricted to only the above average group, but can be found in individuals with normal or below average intelligence. Many retarded persons even in the trainable mentally retarded range (35 to 50 IQ) have demonstrated great talents through the medium of art or music. In Los Angeles the Exceptional Children Foundation maintains a special art center for exceptional children, including the retarded. Some paintings made by trainable retarded adolescents have been sold for as much as several hundred dollars. In the center the children also do extremely beautiful work with charcoal, finger paint, ceramics, and sculpture. Many trainable and educable (50 to 75 IQ) mentally retarded persons also have done exceedingly well in music. In some institutions in this country the retarded have not only mastered playing musical instruments, but they have formed bands and orchestras. Some of these groups have performed on television before national audiences. In addition to special talents in art and music, some persons in the retarded range have mechanical and electrical aptitudes and have learned to make repairs to machines and appliances; others have shown physical prowess in such athletic endeavors as boxing, baseball, track, and swimming.

We can readily see the dangers of conceiving of intelligence as a monolithic quality or as an IQ measure alone, especially when we consider what has just been said. We also have to wonder about all the talent that was not developed because of the previous false assumptions of intelligence. We have learned that creativity and special talents are not solely limited to children with three digits in their IQs.

The impact of the studies and writings of Piaget, Bruner, J. Guilford, J. McV. Hunt, and I. Gordon on intelligence, cognitive growth, learning, and experience are rapidly changing the earlier conception that intelligence is fixed and predetermined. The kinds of schools that operated on the basis of this notion are rapidly changing and in the near future will no longer exist. These mechanistic, fixed Newtonian views of children and schools are shifting to a more Einsteinian view in which intellectual development is seen as open-ended and modifiable in both sequence and rate and intelligence is seen as modifiable. We can examine the change from a Newtonian to an Einsteinian world through the corresponding shifts in the assumptions about man and his development that are now occurring rapidly, and those still to come (Gordon, 1966). The following diagram[2] schematizes the two models.

Newtonian Model Man	*Einsteinian Model Man*
A mechanistic, fixed, closed system, characterized by:	An open-energy, self-organizing system, characterized by:
(1) fixed intelligence	(1) modifiable intelligence
(2) development as an orderly unfolding	(2) development as modifiable in both rate and sequence

2. From Ira J. Gordon, *Studying the Child in School,* John Wiley & Sons, Inc., 1966, p. 2. Printer with permission of the publisher.

(3) potential as fixed, although indeterminable	(3) potential as creatable through transaction with environment
(4) a telephone-switchboard brain	(4) a computer brain
(5) a steam-engine driven motor	(5) a nuclear power-plant energy system
(6) homeostatic regulator (drive-reduction)	(6) inertial guidance and self-regulatory feedback-motivation system
(7) inactive until engine is stoked	(7) continuously active

The Einsteinian view incorporates Piaget's characterization of development as an adaptive process in that the child is constantly modifying the environment and the environment is continuously forcing the child to adapt himself to the given situation. The Einsteinian notion, however, is a transactional one in which the child is not seen as a separate entity apart from his environment, from society, or from his cultural experience. This new approach differs from the interactional model in that the interactional model implies the operation of two or more independent entities. In the transactional approach we must consider that at any given moment in time, when an individual is engaged with another individual or an event, both exist only in terms of each other and behavior cannot be understood apart from the situation, including both temporal and spatial aspects, in which it occurs. For example, in a family the parents shape the child, the child shapes his parents, and the children shape each other and their parents, depending on the kinds of transactions.

In a school the behaviors of the teachers, children, principal, and parents are changed by moment-to-moment dealings with each other. Thus, the behavior of any group or the individuals in the group cannot be understood apart from the situation. During the transaction, the human being can perceive his own feedback or output. Much of learning and development is based on recognizing the effects of one's responses or behavior. This important principle is the underlying reinforcement for learning and for modifying development.

It is in this transactional model that the child responds to the teacher in some way. The child realizes that his response allows him to perceive what he is doing and also what is occurring in the entire sequence. The teacher, by presenting the task or engaging in the event with the child, is also receiving feedback, as are the other pupils. For example, if the child is physically active, such as playing basketball, or academically active, such as spelling a word or doing a math problem, he is monitoring his own behavior, as are all the other persons in the transactional model. The child, however, is also monitoring the new input as a perception of its affect on the teacher and the other children. How is what I am doing affecting the teacher? Am I obtaining the approval from the teacher and the children to the extent I expect for this kind of behavior? How can I or how should I modify my behavior to obtain the approval from the teacher? If I modify my response or behavior, what kind of reaction would I get from the teacher? From the pupils?

When presenting the task to the child, the teacher must determine what kind of a behavioral or performance response or outcome he desires. The teacher should monitor his own role and behavior to establish with the child the consequences for certain types of responses. The appropriate or correct response will be rewarded or reinforced, the inappropriate or wrong response may very well be ignored completely, and the teacher may model the appropriate response together with the pupil. The teacher will have to raise basic questions in the monitoring of the learning situation; so, at that very moment he is also monitoring the way he presents the task or problem and may raise these questions: How is the child or learner receiving it? In what way is he monitoring the imput of the new perception, and what impact or effect does it have on the child? To what extent is he matching the desired outcome? What kinds of different approaches or strategies do I as a teacher need to apply to obtain the desired outcome? These and many other monitoring questions or feedback must be constantly assessed by the teacher. Through this process learning takes place and reinforcements produce the desired outcome (B. Gardner, 1971).

An important part of the transactional model is that the newer concept of intellectual development has to do with the nature of readiness for learning and what determines this readiness. A former notion about mental processes in children was that readiness occurred as a function of physiological maturation. For example, at six most normal children are ready to begin reading. If their intelligence is lower than average, then perhaps at seven or eight they will be ready to begin the three Rs. The new approach on cognitive development says that development is modifiable in both rate and sequence, and we therefore have a responsibility to make children ready. We no longer have to wait for readiness to result from biological maturation. Piaget and Bruner have said that we create readiness by providing experiences for the child that are just one-half step from where he is right now. The task of the teacher or parent then is to accelerate the onset of readiness and enhance the growth of intelligence. No longer can he simply turn to the child development expert and ask him when the child is ready or how bright or how dull the child is.

> All this means that schooling, instruction, and education will not be of maximum effectiveness if we adopt either of two extreme views—that readiness for learning depends simply upon the passage of time or that it is ever present "at any age." We cannot simply wait for pupils to maturate. We must provide for, produce, or build, both cognitive and noncognitive readiness. In so doing we shall directly and deliberately improve teaching and learning. (Tyler, 1964, p. 239)

In other words, no longer is it necessary to sit and wait for intelligence to develop. Intelligence is a modification, revision, and reorganization of what is present. Piaget and Bruner have given us a great deal to think about in the construction of readiness in a child. Although Bruner sees cognitive growth and development in a somewhat different way than Piaget, they both believe we no longer should wait for a child to mature to give the experiences, but we must now participate in making the child ready for the experience in order to enhance and accelerate the onset of his next step or level in mental functioning.

In utilizing the Einsteinian model man or the transactional view we now must not only think in terms of the learner, his potential, and so on, but we also should examine the potential and development of the teacher. The teacher's values, attitudes, training, experiences, motivation, and a whole host of factors, all known as his concepts, will greatly influence the learning situation and the outcome.

For success in promoting child growth and learning, the teacher should have adopted this transactional model in his philosophy concerning children and their development. The teacher then must draw knowledge heavily from both the behavioral sciences and from educational research. We know that the concepts a teacher holds are derived from his particular organization and integration of knowledge and thus influence his perceptions and transactions (Gordon, 1964). In the classroom the impact of the transactions on the learning situation would be great because the teacher, the child, the pupils, and the events only exist in terms of each other.

One major task of the teacher in the transactional model is to understand fully the factors under his control that influence development and growth. J. McV. Hunt in his paper in this book suggests strongly that we should think of psychological development and of intelligence as a hierarchy of learning sets, strategies of information processing, concepts, motivational systems, and skills acquired in the course of each child's ongoing interaction, and especially informational interaction with his environmental circumstances. He further stresses that readiness is no mere matter of maturation that takes place automatically at a certain age; rather, it is a matter of information stored; of concepts, strategies, and motivational systems achieved; and of skills acquired. The teacher's task, then, is to accelerate readiness in the child by solving what Hunt (1961) labeled as the "problem of the match."

> On the side of practice, this notion of a proper match between circumstance and schema is what every teacher must grasp, perhaps only intuitively, if he is to be effective. It was such a match that "Teacher" extraordinary Anne Sullivan sought and found when she pumped water on Helen Keller's (1903) hand as she

> spelled the word into her hand and "got across" the learning set that "things have names" [p. 268].

He cautions that "inasmuch as experience and maturation are constantly changing the schemata[3] of the child, there must be a continual concern with the appropriateness of the match in order to maximize the enrichment of an environment" (p. 272).

The following principles (Gordon, 1966) are some of the concepts the teacher must remember:

1. In any level or phase of cognitive development, the child's learning behavior is a function of the structure and its parts, the organization and integration he has already developed, the nature of the immediate learning task, and the manner in which the task is presented.

    a. If the task does not "match" the child's schemata of development, he will not actively engage in the mastery of the task.

    b. Failure to engage the child in the learning of the task may be due to mismatching in several dimensions. The task may be too difficult for the child because it may be too many steps beyond his present cognitive structure and developmental level or it may be too easy for the child and fails to challenge his competitive motivation.

2. The task may be mismatched because it is emotionally threatening to the child's ego or too far removed from his basic psychological needs.

    a. If the task is seen by the child as meeting his level of

---

3. In the specific sense, schemata are the sensorimotor equivalents of concepts in that they permit the infant to deal economically with different objects of the same class and with different states of the same object. In the general sense, schemata are the structures at any level of mental development.

aspirations and goals and if it is presented at the child's appropriate cognitive level, then the child will actively engage in mastering it.

b. The teacher must realize that both the interaction of the cognitive and affective variables is constantly involved in the child's learning development.

3. The mastery of a new task or a proper match changes the schemata of the child.

   a. Cognitive structure in a person is built upon the successive mastery of means by which to acquire and utilize knowledge presented by the environment.

   b. Motivation and the self-concept or self-image, the concept that one is competent and confident, is derived also from the mastery of new learning tasks.

Thus, teaching children, including those who are retarded, can be viewed as a very complex and complicated process. The teacher must be well prepared by education and by experience to accelerate the rate of growth and sequence of the development of the retarded. For success in the educational process, the teacher must have a very positive philosophy about children and their growth. The motivation and concepts of the teacher will have an important influence on the ultimate outcome. In utilizing the transactional approach, the teacher will have to develop sets of strategies—different ways of presenting tasks and arranging the curriculum in small, logical, sequential learning units. Inasmuch as the behavior of the teacher is influenced by and influences the growth and development of the pupil, it is of vital importance that the teacher develop various patterns of behavior responses for use with the children. To further enhance the learning situation, the teacher must monitor the effect her behavior has on the transactions. Accordingly, she must modify or select the appropriate behavior pattern as required.

Thus, the teacher in preparing the lesson, in applying the various strategies, and in presenting the learning tasks to the pupils should consider not only the basic principles of learning and child development but also the specific information about each retarded pupil in the class.

In the chapters written by Zigler, Elkind, and Hunt there is much information to aid the teacher of the retarded. D. Elkind in his chapter "Border-line Retardation in Low and Middle Income Adolescents" discusses the wide variety of young people who fall within the mild retardation range and conveys clearly the approaches, especially the "classroom climate" for the individuals in each category or group. In the chapter entitled, "Psychological Assessment, Developmental Plasticity, and Heredity, With Implications for Early Education," Hunt discusses the importance of the self-concept, especially the ideal self-concept, the issue of motivational autonomy, and he gives suggestions for fostering the retarded's intellectual and motivational development. Zigler in "Why Retarded Children Do Not Perform Up to the Level of Their Ability" shares with us his voluminous studies of research into the areas of cognition, motivation, and outer-directedness. Throughout this chapter the teacher of the retarded will find valuable insights and suggestions on how to work with retarded children of different backgrounds and experience. Zigler believes that an understanding of the role of affective, motivational, and personality factors and their relation to the intellectual level will help us better understand why the retarded do not perform up to their level of cognitive ability, or why teachers fail in their efforts to educate the retarded. Zigler offers several different ways in which we might help them attain their level of cognitive ability. He suggests that our efforts to optimize the behavior of the retarded would be enhanced if we changed their learned motivational patterns. Finally, he feels that within the area of social behavior we can do a great deal more to enhance the retarded person's everyday effectiveness and social adjustment.

To make the proper match in circumstance and schema the teacher must be able to diagnose and assess the children to determine their present stage of development. What are the cognitive styles of the children? What are their ways of approaching problems? What would motivate the children with respect to problems, tasks, and materials? How do the children organize and integrate their information about the world? How and at what level do the children transact with others? What are the children's ideas about themselves? What are their aspirations and goals? How adequate are these goals in dealing effectively with the world? These questions should be raised in terms of the group and with respect to each pupil in the group.

Diagnostic procedures based on cognitive models of development suggest that the teacher's diagnosis of the pupils' capabilities should involve a systematic examination of the following processes (Strother, 1966):

1. Motor ability and level of functioning, such as coordination, dexterity, equilibrium and laterality, and directionality

2. Perceptual ability and level of functioning in the various sensory modalities, such as visual, tactile, kinesthetic, and auditory

3. Perceptual-motor ability and the level of functioning in the various perceptual-motor areas, such as the copying of figures, writing, and so on

4. Memory ability and recall

5. Ability in the areas of symbolization, concept formation, abstract thinking level, and problem solving

6. Motivational level

7. Linguistic ability and response formation

The teacher of the retarded should certainly become very familiar with the various psychodiagnostic instruments that are available today to aid in the diagnostic evaluation of the learner, for example, the Illinois Test of Psycholinguistic Abilities, the Mariane Frostig Developmental Test of Visual Perception, and others, including tests of social development and motivation.

Another important task for the teacher is to continuously assess the program structure to ascertain what type and level of material should be present and in what way this material should be presented. Is the child able to receive it, develop concepts from it, and utilize the concepts in a meaningful and useful way? For facilitating these goals, the curriculum should be appropriately arranged for the teacher in logical sequential steps. Each step should become the proper match for the child in his "ladder of growth" in development.

In teaching the retarded through the transactional approach we have presented the importance of the environmental structure, the structure of the teaching materials, and the educational program structure to ensure the proper match. Lastly, the teacher has to be concerned about the classroom milieu and the peer organization of the class. This aspect of teaching the retarded is very important. The teacher must be sensitive to the ego level or development of each child to maintain positive interpersonal relations with each child and the children as a group. To help the child's personality growth and his feelings and attitudes toward himself and others, the teacher must be aware of the child's inner and outer worlds. The teacher will have to appraise the habitual attitudes and patterns of defense the child has acquired over the years. In short, the teacher should expect to be an "ego bank" so that he can provide the retarded pupil with real achievements, a sense of accomplishment and self-respect, a sense of trust and initiative. The proper relations will ensure that the child has the opportunities to develop cognitive and other skills that would otherwise remain nascent.

References

Allen, R., & Cortazzo, A. *Psychosocial and educational aspects and problems of mental retardation.* Springfield, Ill.: Charles C Thomas, 1970.

Allen, R., Cortazzo, A., & Toister, R. (Eds.) *The role of genetics in mental retardation.* Coral Gables, Fla.: University of Miami Press, 1971.

Bruner, J., Goodnow, J., & Austin, G. *A study of thinking.* New York: John Wiley & Sons, 1956.

Bruner, J., Olver, R., and Greenfield, P., et al. *Studies in cognitive growth.* New York: John Wiley & Sons, 1966.

Bruner, J. *Toward a theory of instruction.* Cambridge, Mass.: Harvard University Press, 1966.

Flavell, J. *The developmental psychology of Jean Piaget.* Princeton, N.J.: Van Nostrand, 1963.

Gardner, B. Language, intellectual, and cognitive attributes. In *For Young Children.* New Jersey: Project Quest, 1971.

Gardner, R. The needs of teachers for specialized information on the development of cognitive structures. In W. Cruickshank (Ed.), *The teacher of brain-injured children: A discussion of the bases for competency.* Syracuse: Syracuse University Press, 1966.

Gordon, I. *Studying the child in school.* New York: John Wiley & Sons, 1966.

Guilford, J. *The nature of human intelligence.* New York: McGraw-Hill, 1967.

Hunt, J. *Intelligence and experience.* New York: Ronald Press, 1961.

Hunt, J. Intrinsic motivation and its role in psychological development. In *Nebraska symposium on motivation.* Lincoln, Neb.: University of Nebraska Press, 1965.

Inhelder, B., & Piaget, J. The growth of logical thinking. In *Childhood to Adolescence.* New York: Basic Books, 1958.

Kephart, N. *The slow learner in the classroom.* Columbus, Ohio: Charles E. Merrill Books, 1966.

Osborn, D. K. Personal-social attributes of children from birth to eight years. In *For Young Children.* New Jersey: Project Quest, 1971.

Piaget, J. *Six psychological studies.* New York: Random House, 1967.

Rappaport, S. Personality factors teachers need for relationship structure. In W. Cruickshank (Ed.), *The teacher of brain-injured children: A discussion of the bases for competency.* Syracuse: Syracuse University Press, 1966.

Robinson, H., & Robinson, N. *The mentally retarded child: A psychological approach.* New York: McGraw-Hill, 1965.

Sears, P., & Hilgard, E. The teacher's role in the motivation of the learner. In *Theories of learning and instruction.* Chicago: National Society for the Study of Education, 1964.

Sears, P., & Sherman, V. *In pursuit of self-esteem: Case studies of eight elementary school children.* Belmont, Calif.: Wadsworth Publishing Company, 1964.

Strother, S. The needs of teachers for specialized information in the area of psychodiagnosis. In W. Cruickshank (Ed.), *The teacher of brain-injured children: A discussion of the bases for competency.* Syracuse: Syracuse University Press, 1966.

Torrance, P. *Guiding creative talent.* Englewood Cliffs, N.J.: Prentice-Hall, 1962.

Tyler, F. Issues related to readiness to learn. In *Theories of Learning and Instruction.* Chicago: National Society for the Study of Education, 1964.

Wallach, M., & Kogan, N. *Modes of thinking in young children.* New York: Holt, Rinehart & Winston, 1965.

White, R. *Motivation reconsidered: The concept of competence.* Psychology Review, 1959, **66**, 297-333.

Wylie, R. *The self-concept.* Lincoln, Neb.: University of Nebraska Press, 1961.

David Elkind

Border-line Retardation in Low and Middle Income Adolescents

OF ALL THE LEVELS of mental retardation, the diagnoses of "border-line" retardation, roughly IQs in the sixties and low seventies, are the most difficult to make and to interpret. These diagnoses are particularly difficult to determine for young people from minority subcultures whose values, language, and orientations are not adequately represented on mental tests. In the case of these young people, and of many middle income youth as well, the issue of border-line intelligence merges with the broader issues of the validity of mental testing and ethnic differences in intellectual ability.

Before proceeding it is important to say that I will be writing here primarily as a clinician and not as an experimental investigator. For over ten years I have been working with delinquent youth, many of whom fall in the border-line category. Accordingly, the discussion is built upon my experience with adolescents who test at the border-line level. In the first section I describe some varieties of border-line retardation found among middle and low income adolescents. In the next section I review and evaluate some of the "deprivation theories" that have been offered to explain border-line retardation among low income youth. The final

David Elkind, Ph.D., is a professor of psychology in the Department of Psychology, University of Rochester, New York.

section introduces some developmental constructs that provide alternative explanations for test retardation among low income youth.

Varieties of Border-line Retardates

In clinical practice one meets a wide variety of different young people who fall within the border-line IQ category. Such young people can, however, be placed within a few more or less distinctive categories. Easiest to diagnose are the prima facie retardates whose language and behavior give an impression of retardation which is then confirmed by test results. Such retardates are found among both low and middle income young people. More difficult to diagnose are those adolescents whose manner and language are not suggestive of retardation but who nonetheless perform at that level. Such test retardates manifest different patterns usually according to income level. Middle income test retardates tend to be "anxious" or "liberated" whereas low income retardates tend to be "negativistic" or "ingratiating." We need now to look at each of these groups in a little more detail.

Prima Facie Border-line Retardation

A fairly typical pattern among prima facie border-line retardates is that they are exploited by friends and companions into stealing or other delinquent acts. When they come to the court clinic they are generally friendly and affable but fairly limited in vocabulary and in ability to express themselves. Such young people are usually open and friendly and quite eager to be liked, a trait that often gets them into trouble.

Many of these adolescents are quite sensitive about their limited intellectual abilities. Clinically this sensitivity can be seen in a reaction which is very typical of this group of border-line retardates and which is usually absent among young people with higher IQs. When confronted with the first few easy items on the information subtest of the WISC, the prima facie border-line retardate almost invariably laughs at such items as "from what animal do we get milk?" The dynamics are clear enough. A young person with limited ability is very anxious about his intellectual prowess and fears he will reveal himself on the test. The first few easy questions flood him with relief, which is then expressed in laughter. Rather typical of this group, too, is their failure to really listen to the instructions and to fully appreciate that the succeeding questions will get harder.

Border-line retardates of the prima facie variety present very special problems of placement and education. Although it is clear that they need special academic programs, it is not clear what the nature of these programs should be. I do not want to enter the debate as to whether such young people should be placed in special classes or kept with their age mates. Both programs have advantages and disadvantages. The really crucial factor is the attitude of the people involved. Special classes in a total school climate that is warm and accepting will not make the children in those classes feel stigmatized. Likewise, handled with acceptance and consideration, border-line students can be integrated within a regular classroom. What counts is always the orientation of the people involved, not the structure of the program.

Middle Income Test Retardates

In talking about middle income test retardates, I am clearly not talking exclusively about white teenagers inasmuch as middle income black youths demonstrate patterns comparable to those manifested by the whites. It is important to remember that the black community is every bit as diversified, variegated, and full of conflict as the white community. In the clinic setting, socioeconomic level can be every bit as significant as race in determining behavior patterns. Accordingly, one sees the liberated and anxious patterns described in this section among middle-class youth from many different ethnic backgrounds. What they have in common is the incorporation of the middle-class value system.

The liberated. The typical liberated young person comes for testing dressed in loose fitting, shapeless clothes and presents a rather uncombed and ungroomed appearance. Such young people are quite often defiant in a quiet and non-physical way, and it soon becomes clear that they are fighting the system and not just the examiner. They are interested in the tests, but are quite ready to take umbrage at the questions. Indeed, the reason that liberated young people do poorly on the tests is that they often disagree with the values expressed in test questions, such as "Why should criminals be locked up?" and "Why should women and children be saved first in a shipwreck?" The young people may reply that criminals should not be locked up and women should not always be saved before men. These answers are, of course, not given any credit. In many ways, therefore, the liberated young person approaches the standard intelligence test as if it were a measure of divergent or creative thinking and gives a poor showing. The poor showing is in itself an expression of distaste for a social system that places value on measured intelligence.

How shall such a performance be interpreted? Clearly it does not reflect the young person's true intellectual potential or even his current level of mental functioning; but rather, it reflects his attitude toward conformity and toward conventional demands. As such the test data, taken together with the clinical evidence of near-average intelligence, are still significant. They reveal why, for example, such young people often fail in school, why they cannot get along with their parents, and why they live with friends rather than go to work. The performance of these young people on intelligence tests is a reflection of their life-style, of their apparent rejection of generally accepted societal standards and values including mental testing and academic achievement. The question is whether such rejection is more apparent than real.

In the first place we must emphasize that not all liberated young people perform poorly on intelligence tests. Just those persons, I suspect, who have low average ability go to extremes in their intelligence test performance. Their rejection of the tests is an attempt to deny that they place any value on intellectual ability. By denying that test intelligence has value, they no longer have to feel ashamed of their own limited ability. Such young people often fool themselves into believing that their rejection of society and its values is genuine. In fact, of course, it is just as likely that they have rejected society before it has had a good chance to reject them. If they are open to it, some of these young people can be helped with counseling. But their parents must be counseled too, for unless parents can bring their demands into line with their children's modest abilities, counseling may well be undermined and sabotaged from the start.

The anxious. The young person who performs at the borderline level because of extreme anxiety is a much less frequent occurrence than the liberated young person. Among the anxious group, the causes of anxiety are quite diverse. One young woman who came in for testing was still mourning her father's death four years after his death. Her depression and anxiety severely inhibited her test performance. A different type of case recently came to my attention. A fifteen-year-old adolescent girl who was slender and attractive and who did not appear to be intellectually retarded from her speech or interpersonal behavior had been having headaches and fainting spells. An abnormal pattern was reported when EEGs were taken. Although the girl did not tell me so, she was terribly concerned about losing her intellectual powers and probably had some intimation of such with lapses of memory and so on. While taking the WISC she repeatedly blocked because of her anxiety and attained a verbal IQ score of 61.

One could object, of course, that such testing is invalid and that the obtained score is spurious and of no value. Although this objection needs to be raised, I cannot agree with the uselessness of the testing. Even though I realized that the girl was anxious about the testing, nothing in her appearance or manner suggested the extent of the blocking that actually occurred. Since I tried very hard to make the testing a comfortable and nonanxious situation, the extent of blocking is significant. It certainly helps explain why she is failing in school and pinpoints a major focus of her anxiety, namely, her concern over failing intellectual abilities. Calling this girl retarded would be foolish, but throwing out the diagnostic significance of her performance would be equally foolish. In most cases adolescents who fall in this anxious category are very much in need of professional guidance and psychotherapy. It is important that school personnel be made aware of the young person's special problems and that the personnel be given guidance as to how to best help the anxious adolescent.

Low Income Test Retardates

Perhaps the most frequent and diagnostically difficult cases of border-line retardation are the many young people who come from ethnic and economic backgrounds other than those presupposed by most of our mental tests. Within this group are low income blacks, Spanish-speaking teenagers, and white youth from poverty areas. When these teenagers come in for testing, they present one of two contrasting patterns, negativism or ingratiation. Sometimes the same person will show both patterns at different times.

Regardless of whether the young person is negativisitic or ingratiating, one common characteristic that stands out in the testing situation is the language differences between the middle income examiner and the lower income examinee. Not only are there differences in articulation, vocabulary, and inflection, but there are also more subtle differences in phrasing and emphasis. The communication problem is a very real one that complicates testing and diagnosis.

On the WISC, for example, a black male may refuse to define the word "spade" because it happens to be a slang word for a black man. Or a low income youngster may say something like "Humb" that turns out to be Humboldt Avenue, the street on which he lives. Sometimes the misunderstanding can be amusing, as in the case of the young person who makes a face when he hears "espionage" as "spinach." These language differences are very apparent to the examinee as well as to the examiner, and they pose an additional barrier to effective rapport and valid testing. In my own work I find that it is important to confront the issue directly, to restate words I feel have not been understood, and to have the adolescent repeat words I could not comprehend. If the young person realizes the examiner really wants to understand him and is not making aspersions about his speech, such little confrontations can be most helpful in aiding communication. Minor confrontations are equally effective with negativistic and ingratiating adolescents.

The negativistic adolescent. A great many low income adolescents come in for testing in a rather surly mood. They tend to feel that someone thinks that they are crazy and that tests will be used against them in one way or another. They are also secretly afraid of tests as if the tests had some magical power to do things to them or to find out things about them that they do not wish to be known. The negativism is usually expressed directly in overt outbursts of anger at the examiner and diatribes against the tests—"that ole stupid stuff"—or in a sullen, unbending silence.

Examples of some typical young people of this kind may help to make their negativism more concrete. One case was a fourteen-year-old, well-developed black male who came to the testing against his will. He refused to take the tests saying that he would not answer "them damn questions." After his probation officer spoke to him for a few moments he agreed to participate but with reluctance. Of the beginning questions (What must you do to make water boil? etc.) on the WISC he said, "Oh man, that's stupid. Everybody knows that." His anger increased as the items became more difficult, and he finally turned away and said, "I ain't gonna answer no more of that sh—!" As with most cases of this kind, I discontinued testing and made another appointment. Almost without exception negativisitic young people are much more cooperative on the second testing. It is as if having succeeded in stopping the testing the first time, they have made their point and do not need to make it again.

An example of another kind of negativism was given by a fifteen-year-old, a small, well-proportioned black girl. She came in, sat down, and said nothing in response to my greeting and initial structuring of the testing. (I routinely introduce myself, explain that I am going to give some tests, and ask whether the adolescent has ever had tests before.) After answering a few questions on the WISC she seemed unable to answer one of the questions. When I went on to the next question she continued silent. No matter what I said or how I encouraged her, she sat looking into her lap and not talking. Again, as in the case of the aggressively negativistic adolescent, I terminated testing and set another appointment. When she returned a week later she was cooperative, and she completed the tests without incident.

It should be said, perhaps, that the negativism shown by these young people is, to a large extent, culturally stereotyped. Many of these young people complain that they have a headache or are tired or that they do not feel well. Often such ploys seem to be well-learned modes of avoiding activities in which the adolescents do not want to participate. Once this behavior is set in motion, as I indicated earlier, it is difficult to do much about other than to let it run its course and to try again another day. Not surprisingly, these negativistic patterns seem to date back to slavery days when such techniques were constantly used to get back at the "man" (Bernard, 1966).

The ingratiating adolescent. Much less frequent than the negativistic adolescent is the adolescent who is ingratiating in attitude and manner. Such young people come into the testing situation looking frightened and threatened. They obey requests as if they are commands and seem to be searching for cues to the right response in the examiner's facial expression and behavior. Some ingratiating adolescents are rather outgoing and jovial, but they still reflect the eagerness to please and the fear of offending that seem to characterize this group of young people.

This pattern of behavior appears to be a cultural stereotype adopted by those adolescents who find being aggressive difficult and need some mode of relating to authority. Underneath the ingratiation is not only fear but also hostility, which sometimes comes through in a chance or unguarded remark. The ingratiating pattern probably dates back to the days of slavery when such patterns were the blacks' only defense against the dominant authority of whites; but, it may be more general than that, for white young people show the ingratiating and negativistic patterns too.

The intellectual performance of the low income test retardate, whether the negativistic or ingratiating type, tends to show much scatter. Consider the pattern of the negativistic young man described earlier. He did poorly on tests of information, vocabulary, and arithmetic, but he did much better on tests of comprehension and similarities (which tend to measure ability more than content whereas the reverse is true for the other tests). His verbal IQ was 68 and his performance IQ was ten points higher. The full scale IQ was 73. On the Rorschach, the number and quality of the human responses were suggestive of low-average to average intellectual ability. His figure drawings, in contrast, were poor, suggesting less than average ability. My clinical impression was that his potential level of ability was at least in the low-average range. This pattern of performance, and the clinical impression of higher ability than that suggested by the attained test scores, is, in my experience, common to low income test retardates.

Another common factor in this group is an outspoken hatred of school. We should emphasize that this hatred is more than lip service to a popular and conventional attitude of the high school culture. Most of the teen-agers who say they hate school (but who attend regularly) really like the social world the school affords. But the low income test retardates are habitual truants who hate school with a genuine passion. It is a place where they have experienced repeated failure, ridicule, and embarrassment. Many of these young people have developed an antipathy to formal education of any kind. One reason for the negativism of so many of these young people is that the examiner in some respects is the embodiment of the formal educational establishment they so despise.

In recent years the low income test retardate has come into the spotlight as a consequence of the civil rights movement. The poor intellectual and academic performances by low income youth have been used as arguments for much social and educational legislation. School integration and such programs as Head Start have been introduced to equalize the educational opportunities of low and middle income young people. Such programs presuppose that the test retardation of low income youth is primarily a function of intellectual deprivation and that providing adequate intellectual nourishment will greatly remediate the problem.

Other theories, in addition to the deprivation theory, have been offered to explain the test retardation of many low income youth. My argument against such theories is that those who propound them usually work from data collected in large-scale survey studies. When one works directly with young people, however, the validity of the information and the conclusions drawn from such large-scale studies seem highly questionable because interpretations of data are only as good as the data itself. My own feeling is that much large-scale data on low income youth are probably not very reliable. In the next section I want to look more closely at some of the theories that have been propounded to explain the test retardation of low income youth. Particularly I want to look at the theories from the standpoint of the clinician who works on a one-to-one basis with the young people represented by the statistic.

Theories of Test Retardation Among Low Income Youth

It is probably fair to say that the extant theories of test retardation among low income youth tend to be "deficit" models. Such models presuppose that low income youth are deficient in (a) inherited ability, (b) intellectually enriching experiences, (c) appropriate motivation and interpersonal skills, or (d) adequate nutrition. After reviewing these theories, I would like to suggest some alternative explanations that derive from clinical and developmental considerations.

Test Retardation as a Reflection of Limited Genetic Endowment

In a recent controversial article A. R. Jensen (1969) reviewed the extensive literature on the test intelligence of black and white young people. He noted that blacks routinely score lower than whites on IQ tests and that this difference holds true even when socioeconomic level is held constant. He concluded that there is a genetic difference between blacks and whites and that blacks are more endowed with associative abilities and whites are more endowed with abstract abilities. Even more recently R. Hernnstein (1971) seems to have taken a position rather close to Jensen's.

Both Jensen (1969) and Hernnstein (1971) have been criticized from many different points of view, and I do not wish to review all those criticisms here. Rather, I would like to approach the question from the standpoint of the testing itself. What has to be emphasized is that the administration of individual or group intelligence tests involves a number of biases. Such biases involve much more than the fact that some of the test items may be inappropriate to the low income adolescent's experience. As the evidence presented in the following suggests, the total testing context is the one that affects test performance, and this context is often radically different for low income than for middle income children. Such context effects enter into both individual and group testing and make it hazardous to use the results of such testing to make inferences about inherited abilities. Let us consider those context effects in individual and group testing.

In the earlier discussion of the mental assessment of low income test retardates I suggested some of the difficulties inherent in a middle-class examiner working with a low income examinee. The problems of communication and of cultural stereotypes are, however, only part of the problem. Studies suggest, for example, that black children perform better when tested by a black examiner than when tested by a white examiner (Canady, 1936; Forrester & Klaus, 1964). It is probably fair to say that a good many of the studies used to demonstrate race or income differences in intelligence involve examiners and examinees of different races and social class.

Another related factor in individual testing was recently demonstrated by E. Zigler and E. C. Butterfield (1968) with Head Start children. One finding of the study was that when the same children were given an individual intelligence test under maximizing (warm, supportive, relaxed, encouraging) and standard (cool, objective, nonreinforcing) conditions, an average difference of ten points occurred in favor of the test taken under maximizing conditions. Another finding was that a comparable change occurred between standard testing of children before and after their attendance at a Head Start program. These results suggest that when Head Start programs produce IQ changes in children the programs do not change mental ability per se. Rather, what is more likely is that Head Start programs change the test orientation of low income children. By the end of a Head Start program, children are comfortable with middle income adults and with examination procedures. In short, one might say that Head Start makes children more motivated, comfortable, and attentive test takers.

The motivational factor is, however, but one of the contextual factors that enter into a child's performance on an individual test of intelligence. Cultural values and ethics also enter into such performance. A case in point is reflected in an unpublished study I conducted with the Ogalala Sioux of Pine Ridge, South Dakota. I wanted to get normative data on some tests of perceptual development (Elkind, 1969) which my students and I developed over the years. The Sioux live in a perceptually barren part of the country (near the badlands of South Dakota) and in a relatively isolated and perceptually impoverished environment insofar as such things as books, paintings, etc., are concerned. Their performance on perceptual tests might reflect the importance of culturally provided perceptual experience for success on our tests.

Initially, the results of the testing were what I had (I confess) hoped to find. That is, the Sioux youngsters did much worse on tests of figure-ground reversal and part-whole integration than our middle- and lower-class Anglo norm groups. As a clinician, however, I was dissatisfied with the way in which the children performed, and I suspected that they were not telling me everything that they had seen. I then tried procedures similar to what Zigler and Butterfield (1968) called "maximizing." I spent a lot of time talking to each child, drawing him out and showing that I was genuinely interested in his performance. With such procedures the children suddenly came out of their shells and performed as well or better than our middle and low income white children.

I discovered when I explored this situation with some of the Indian teachers that I was dealing with cultural and interpersonal values. First, I found that most of the children are self-conscious about their Indian names (e.g., Chief Running Fast White Water) and are afraid of being ridiculed. Secondly, the Indian culture is basically noncompetitive; indeed, competition is looked at rather negatively. Consequently, Indian children, even the brightest ones, do no more than they need to do to get by. To do their best would be to do better than their peers, which is culturally unacceptable. In my "maximizing" procedures I somehow communicated that I respected the Sioux children's names and did not see their enhanced performance as a sign of their competitiveness. Clearly, the effects of such values upon individual test performance of different ethnic groups have to be considered when interpreting test results as a reflection of inherited ability. Many other cultural factors that affect test performance were recently described by Michael Cole and his colleagues (1971).

Another contextual factor is prominent in testing low income adolescents to which I only alluded earlier. This is a cultural factor that, in my experience, seems to be endemic to low income youth regardless of race or ethnic background. By and large, the middle income adolescent, whether or not he admits it, looks at the test as a challenge and overtly or covertly enjoys testing his mettle. He is also concerned about how he comes off in the examiner's eyes. Indeed, even the hostile middle income youth is very much concerned with "impression management."

A good many (but certainly not all) low income youth approach testing in a very different frame of mind. They do not seem to have learned that "good" performance in matters intellectual is what wins adult approval. Consequently they are less "ego involved" with the testing and less concerned with how they appear in adult eyes than middle-class youth. A large number of low income youth probably see the testing situation as yet another instance where they have to find out how little they can do without getting punished (Elkind, 1971). In other words, middle income children are usually motivated to do well on intelligence tests whereas low income children are usually motivated to get by with the minimum possible performance.

If we look at group testing, the contextual factors appear to be as potent as they are in individual testing. Research on the context effects in group testing is, however, just getting under way. R. Rosenthal and L. Jacobsen (1968) argued that teacher expectancy played a considerable role in children's performance on achievement tests. Although other investigators (e.g., Fleming & Auttonen, 1971) have failed to replicate the Rosenthal and Jacobsen study, the Rosenthal work has stimulated research into the many and complex factors that affect performance on group tests.

A recent study of our own (Elkind, Deblinger, & Adler, 1970) highlights one factor in group testing that seems obvious but is seldom taken seriously in administering group tests. This factor is the activity that is interrupted when children are taken for testing. Our hypothesis was that children's performance on a group test would be enhanced if they were taken from an activity (such as social studies) that many children find uninteresting and their performance on a group test would be impaired if they were taken for testing from an interesting activity (like gym). In our study we used group creativity tests and found that the same children were twice as creative, and three times more original, when group testing interrupted an ongoing dull activity than when it interrupted an ongoing interesting activity.

More directly related to the question of low income children are the findings of E. Long (1966). This investigator ran kindergartens for black and white children in the rural South. Some of the children received an "enriched" program. The Stanford Binet showed no gains for any children. The Thurstone Primary Mental Abilities Test (PMA) did, however, reflect gains. There was some suggestion that the black children profited more from enrichment than the white children. Another sort of contextual factor affecting group test performance became manifest in our ongoing evaluation of an innovative inner city school. We have found that children's test performance waxes and wanes, in part, as a reflection of the morale of teachers and administrators. When the funding for the school seemed in jeopardy, performance on group tests was lower than when the future financial support for the school seemed assured.

Other studies could be added to further document the role of contextual factors in individual and group testing. The data that have been offered, however, may suffice to show some of the sources of error in testing low income youth. Such error, it has to be said, is not random but *systematic* and is therefore missed in statistical calculations for random, or error, variance. Because of such systematic sources of error in group and individual testing of middle as well as low income children, the use of these test findings to make assertions about hereditary differences between groups seems hazardous.

It is important to add, however, that I am in no way attempting to deny that intelligence has a large hereditary component. No one can gainsay that individuals vary in intellectual ability any more than one could deny that physical traits have their origin in genetic transmission. But such a vast empirical and conceptual gulf exists between the level of genes, chromosomes, DNA, and so forth and the behavior of a child on a test that a linkage between the two levels of description and analysis must be tenuous at best. It seems to me that psychologists have been much too facile in leaping from correlational data using group tests to inferences about the contribution of heredity. Many intermediary steps must be taken before we can make inferences from complex behavior to gene complexes and the reverse.

In summary, we have looked at evidence for systematic bias in individual and group tests which adversely affects the performance of blacks and low income groups. The existence of these sources of bias and the enormous gap between the genetic and behavioral levels of analyses make questionable hypotheses about genetic differences in test intelligence between the races or socioeconomic groups. Although intelligence undeniably has a large hereditary component, we lack the knowledge to make specific statements about how that genetic potential gets to be realized in intelligence test performance.

Test Retardation as a Result of Deprivation

Perhaps the most prevalent explanation for the relatively poor performance of low income youth on intelligence tests is the concept of deprivation. This concept has, however, been interpreted in several different ways. Perhaps the most common interpretation is that low income children are deprived of adequate verbal and intellectual stimulation, Another interpretation asserts that low income children are deprived emotionally and interpersonally. A final, somewhat different interpretation is that low income young people do poorly on intelligence tests because of nutritional deprivation. Let us look at each of these explanations in turn.

Intellectual deprivation. The concept that low income children are deprived of adequate intellectual stimulation is based on a variety of research findings. Numerous studies, such as the study of R. D. Hess and V. C. Shipman (1965), report that low income mothers do not engage in as much teaching and verbal interplay with their children as do middle income mothers. Likewise, B. Bernstein (1961) has hypothesized that low income families have a more restricted language system than the economically advantaged families, and B. S. Bloom (1964) suggests that the cost to a child who spends his first four years in a deprived intellectual environment—as opposed to an enriched one—is about ten IQ points.

The problem is to define what one means by a rich as opposed to a deprived intellectual environment. In the case of language, for example, Bernstein's hypothesis that the language of blacks is less elaborated than that of whites has been challenged (Baratz, 1969). The language of the blacks now appears to be a dialect of standard English that is every bit as rich in vocabulary, inflection, and grammatical constructions as is the standard English of the whites. It is at least possible that low income mothers are very articulate when instructing their children in things that matter to them, such as how to get along with whites without being brutalized by them.

These considerations make it clear that intellectual deprivation refers to the kind and not to the quantity of stimulation low income children receive. What they are deprived of is the kind of intellectual stimulation that would prepare them to take tests and to do well in public school, both of which have been designed by middle-class whites. At the same time, however, these low income children have not been deprived of the kind of stimulation and enrichment that they need to adapt to their own environment. Deprivation is thus not an accurate term to describe the intellectual experience of low income young people. Their experience is simply different, not necessarily deficient.

This point is important because the deprivation or deficit model has led to compensatory programs aimed at remedying deficits. Not the least of the negative aspects of such programs is the orientation it produces in adult leaders. If children are regarded as deficient, the intellectual skills and abilities that they do have may not be recognized or respected, which further devalues the child's conception of himself and his family.

Let me try to give an analogy from my experience with the White Mountain Apache of Arizona. During a long evening discussion with some young college-trained Apache men,

I learned a great deal about the Apache religion. It has a trinity not unlike that in Christianity. The Indians felt, however, that the missionaries did not take their religion seriously or respect it. So while the Indians went to church, as much for the free food as the service, they went back to their own religion at times of crises. Many Indian soldiers went to the reservation for a "sing" before they were shipped overseas for combat.

I would not be surprised if a good many "deprived" low income children and their parents participate in compensatory programs with the same ambivalence experienced by Indian families attending the missionary's church. In both cases the low income group are ostensibly accepting a value system different from their own, but only because of the rewards involved. My guess is that the effect of compensatory programs will be superficial in any program where those in charge fail to understand and respect the culture and values of the low income children they are attempting to serve.

The idea that low income children are different, rather than deficient, in the kinds of intellectual stimulation they receive is supported by cross-cultural research on Piagetian tasks. Such tasks measure basic concepts about the physical world (space, time, number, mass, weight, volume, right and left, and so on) which are required for successful adaptation. These Piagetian tasks have now been administered to children all over the world who live in widely varying conditions and who come from vastly different backgrounds. And yet, the results are surprisingly uniform. Children in bush Africa attain the same concepts at about the same time as children in Boston or Geneva (cf. Greenfield, 1966; Goodnow, 1969; and Vernon, 1965).

To be sure, some low income groups appear to be somewhat behind middle income groups. Appalachian children are behind Detroit children (Sigel & Mermelstein, 1965) and children from the country are behind children from the city (Peluffo, 1962), but they appear to go through the same sequence of stages and to attain the same abilities. Perhaps some kinds of environments alter the rate of mental growth.

On the other hand, some of the testing factors mentioned earlier may penalize the low income child on Piagetian tasks. I want to emphasize that low income children, by and large, do better on Piagetian tasks than they do on more formal intelligence tests. Here again the implication is that their environments have not deprived them intellectually, but rather caused them to elaborate their abilities in directions other than those taken by mental evaluation in middle income young people.

Finally, one last point has to be made. Social scientists have been guilty during the last decade of creating new stereotypes of low income children that are every bit as pernicious as some of the earlier "poor people" stereotypes. It is important to remember that there are more intact black families than broken ones, that within the low income community there is tremendous diversity. Parents with high aspirations for their children can provide an environment every bit as stimulating as any to be found in a home in the middle-class suburbs. The reverse is also true; many suburban middle-class homes are probably devoid of what educators might call enriching intellectual environments. In talking about low income youth we must be aware of the danger of homogenization, of assuming that every low income child's experience is the same. Individual differences are every bit as varied in low income as in middle income youth.

Motivational and interpersonal deprivation. A number of studies indicate that low income children are more deficient in achievement motivation than are more affluent children (Douvan, 1956; Lott & Lott, 1963; Mussen, Urbano, & Boutourline-Young, 1961). Achievement motivation is certainly crucial to the full elaboration of intellectual abilities and to competent performance on mental tests. Lack of achievement motivation could thus be an important factor in the border-line retardation of low income youth. Such a lack of achievement motivation is certainly consistent with the clinical impression of low income test retardates that I described earlier.

How is achievement motivation instilled in children? Psychoanalytic theory (Elkstein, 1966) suggests an explanation that is consistent with social learning theories, such as those offered by A. Bandura and B. H. Walters (1963). According to analytically oriented writers, a child's motivation for learning academic materials is not intrinsic but derives from his desire to win parental approval through learning. This means that the parents themselves value academic types of learning and provide manifold rewards when their children perform well at school.

Presumably, low income parents are, on the average, less impressed by academic achievement than middle-class parents. It is certainly true that low income parents may have high aspirations for their children (want them to go to college and so on) yet have rather low expectations (expect that they will work in gas stations and so on). Such parents are not likely to demonstrate in their own behavior a taste for matters intellectual. (They are less likely to read books, magazines, etc.) Hence children are given the message, "Do as I say, not as I do." Moreover, the low income parent may be suspicious of people who are more highly educated than himself and convey this suspicion to his offspring.

Although there is probably considerable truth in these motivational deprivation explanations of test retardation among low income youth, some reservations have to be offered. First, it is important to avoid homogenization and to remember than many low income parents are intellectually motivated whereas many middle income parents are not. Secondly, middle income families are smaller and hence the proportion of first-born and only children is greater than for low income families. First-born children tend to be more competitive and achievement oriented regardless of social class. The apparently greater achievement motivation among middle income families may thus reflect, in part at least, the greater proportion of first-born and only children among this income group.

Nutritional deprivation. In recent years increasing attention has been paid to the role of nutrition in intellectual development. Although much of the research has been done with animals (Barnes, 1968), a number of studies have been done on human populations as well (Cravioto, 1968). Much more research needs to be done, but some tentative conclusions seem reasonably well substantiated.

Apparently the earlier and the more prolonged the nutritional deficiency, the more severe and long-lived are the effects upon physical and mental growth. When pregnant beagles were fed a protein-deficient diet, their pups suffered greater detriment than beagle pups whose mothers had adequate diets during pregnancy. In a study with tribal groups in Africa (Stock & Smyth, 1963) cranial circumference was found to be significantly smaller among children whose mothers ate a nutritionally inadequate diet during pregnancy than among children whose mothers were adequately nourished.

One of the most ambitious studies of nutritional effects upon populations is the longitudinal investigations of J. Cravioto (1968). In his investigations Cravioto looked at the mental test performance of South American children growing up on different diets. In general he concludes that adequacy of nutrition in the early years has a significant long-term effect upon mental ability, alertness, and motivation.

The relevance of these findings to the issue of test retardation in low income adolescents is straightforward. Low income families by definition have relatively little money to spend on food. Protein is, moreover, quite expensive whereas carbohydrates, fats, and starches (bread, potatoes, rice, pasta, and so on) are inexpensive. It is probably fair to say, therefore, that the average low income child has grown up (both prenatally and postnatally) on a less nutritious and balanced diet than the average middle income child. It seems probable that in many cases of low income test retardation a history of prolonged nutritional deficiency probably plays some part.

Developmental Considerations

In the foregoing sections some deprivation models of test retardation among low income youth have been described and critically evaluated. Although such models have some truth, they tend to unduly homogenize and stigmatize the low income groups. The word deprived itself seems to cast aspersions on the quality of nurturance provided by low income families. In fact, low income children are deprived not of intellectual stimulation, but rather, of the kinds of intellectual stimulation that middle income families value and regard as essential to success in our society.

In this connection it is important to recall the relativity of social class values. At one time social scientists described low income mothers as permissive and middle income mothers as strict. Then middle income mothers became more permissive because this attitude was supposed to be good for the child. Consider a more contemporary example. The unwed mother is supposed to be more common among low income women because of their low morals, their ignorance of birth control measures, and so on. But today an unwed mother is the height of chic among middle- and upper-class women. Many well-known women today take pride in the fact that they have had a child out of wedlock. Today's low income disgrace is tomorrow's middle income fashion.

An approach that avoids some of the difficulties of the deprivation models springs from developmental considerations. Stated more directly, how can test retardation be conceived from a developmental perspective? One possibility is that low income youth are retarded or slower in their development than middle income youth. But my clinical impression of low income test retardates suggests two other developmental conceptualizations of these young people. Some low income retardates seem to have intellectual abilities that were *prematurely structured* whereas others have intellectual abilities that have been *alternatively elaborated* in directions other than those taken by intellectual abilities among middle income youth.

Premature Structuring

After one of his lectures, Sigmund Freud was asked whatever became of the shoeshine boys on the street corners of

Vienna and in many other cities. Such young men seemed exceedingly sharp witted, verbal, and socially astute. Freud thought for a moment and replied, "They become cobblers." This story illustrates the phenomena of *premature structuring,*[1] which is by no means limited to low income youth.

By premature structuring I mean that some young people are forced to apply their abilities to practical matters before these abilities are fully realized or elaborated. The effect is to stunt or limit growth. An analogy would be pruning a tree to make it assume a particular shape. Such pruning affects the ultimate limits of tree growth as well as the shape. In the case of low income children the same result may hold true. Out of necessity many such children may have to assume responsibility for their siblings at an early age and to direct their intellectual abilities to practical issues. This early application of mental abilities to real life matters may inhibit future growth.

Certainly many middle-class children have chores (such as mowing the lawn or taking out the garbage) and may even have a paper route. But such chores are usually underwritten and backed by parents (who may even deliver the papers in inclement weather or at least drive their children in automobiles). Middle-class children, however, also engage in many exercises of their mental abilities, such as coin, stamp, and rock collections, games of cards, monopoly, and chess, and other activities, which have no practical end. In this way they exercise mental abilities without forcing them into particular molds.

My guess is that premature structuring is most likely to occur when a child has little or no opportunity to play with his mental abilities. In my opinion such play is crucial to further mental elaboration of abilities (Elkind, 1972). The low income child who has to deal with storekeepers, landlords, little children, bullies, and drunks has to use his abilities in very practical ways, and few low income children

1. Barbara Biber (1959) used this same term to describe the inhibition of creativity in young children when formal education was introduced too early.

have the wherewithal to collect coins, rocks, and stamps or to purchase elaborate games. Because of his practical orientation, the low income child may consider spending time on apparently frivolous games or collections nonsensical. Consequently, academic subjects may seem, to the prematurely structured child, as but another kind of useless play on a par with collecting coins or stamps.

In my clinical experience prematurely structured test retardates show limited interest and seem to focus upon eating, sleeping, working at a job, enjoying a few simple recreations, and nothing else. They show little or no appreciation for such things as politics or even the important community issues that affect them. Such young people seem to live as if they had blinders on which let them pass through life with few distractions. Interpersonally such adolescents come across as narrow and constricted.

Alternate Elaboration

One young man of the ingratiating variety exemplifies the alternate elaboration model of test retardation. He came to the court clinic because he was not going to school and was suspected of pushing dope and of having a couple of girl friends doing "tricks" for him. He was well dressed and smooth talking with a vocabulary rich in the argot of the street and the underworld. He was alternatively amused and annoyed at the test questions, and he did best in arithmetic and worst on the test of general information and vocabulary.

His poor performance on information and vocabulary, however, does not reflect deficiency but rather alternate elaboration. This young man was far from lacking in general information. Indeed, his fund of information in many areas was much greater than mine. The same was true for his vocabulary, which was rich in words not found on intelligence tests. To call this young man deficient in ability would be a gross error. On the contrary, his at least average intellectual abilities were elaborated in a subcultural domain that is virtually unknown to the middle-class test maker and user.

Individuals who manifest alternate elaboration of intellectual abilities are sometimes thought to be malingering. A black adolescent who was not drafted because of his low IQ was taken into custody for running a crap game. When playing craps he demonstrated rather remarkable mathematical acumen in figuring odds. The probation officer was sure this young man had failed the Army IQ test on purpose to avoid the draft. But he failed the intelligence test quite honestly. His mathematical abilities were elaborated in a different way than they are for most young people.

Perhaps a rough analogy will help make the notion of alternate elaboration appear somewhat more plausible. During the first two years of life, the infant's linguistic prowess is infinitely malleable. He will learn any language to which he is systematically exposed. Once he learns a particular language, however, learning a second language becomes progressively more difficult for him as he grows older. After about the age of twelve, according to H. Lennenberg (1967), the critical period for language learning is at end. Possibly something similar occurs in cognitive development. The young man who elaborates his abilities in the underworld subculture acquires a kind of cognitive language that may make it difficult for him to elaborate his abilities or to learn academic material in a traditional school setting.

The concepts of premature structuring and alternate elaboration are offered as alternatives to the various deficit models that have been proposed to account for the test retardation of low income youth. These concepts have been derived primarily from my clinical experience with delinquent young people. They could, however, serve as a starting point for my systematic investigations. In the meantime these concepts of premature structuring and alternate elaboration might prove useful if for no other reason than to divert us from the value-laden terms of deprived and disadvantaged. From a developmental standpoint the mental growth of some low income youth may simply be different in direction and elaboration than that of the offspring of more affluent parents.

Summary and Conclusions

In this paper I have tried to do three things: (a) describe some varieties of border-line retardation observed in clinical practice; (b) critically evaluate some of the theories that have been offered to account for the test retardation in low income youth; and (c) offer an alternative developmental conceptualization of test retardation. In this closing section I want to reemphasize some of the points made earlier and to mention some possible practical implications of the foregoing discussion.

One of the dangers social scientists constantly face is that of homogenization, of treating a group of individuals as if they all exhibited exactly the same traits. It is useful to talk about low and middle income youth and to point out features that are more common to one group than another. But, as I have tried to indicate in this paper, there are wide individual differences within groups. Test retardation appears in both middle income and low income young people although the patterns are somewhat different. Among middle income youth the liberated and anxious syndromes are most common whereas for low income youth the antagonistic and ingratiating are most common.

A second point to be emphasized is the danger of interpreting intelligence test data as a reflector of genetic factors. Although the contribution of heredity to intelligence is assuredly considerable, we are far from understanding the relations between these two very different levels of observation and analysis. Moreover, the many systematic contextual biases that affect the performance of subcultural groups on these tests lessen the usefulness of the tests for inferring group differences in ability. In my opinion, no more reason exists for attributing the test retardation of low income adolescents to heredity than for attributing the test retardation of middle income youth to such genetic factors.

Likewise, since test retardation occurs in both middle and low income youth, environmental deprivation per se is probably not a major factor in test retardation. Rather, what seems to be the case for both middle and low income youth is that test retardation is produced by a complex of individual and social factors, including natural ability, birth order, nutrition, parental motivation, the role models available for imitation, and so on. The complex of factors that make for test retardation may be more common in low income families, but they are certainly not the exclusive province of such families.

From a clinical point of view, the position taken in this paper, large-scale survey studies need to be complemented by clinical investigations which bear witness to the richness and variety of the individual person. This is as true for prima facie retardates as it is for test retardates. From the standpoint of a clinician, an individual is always a person first and a retardate or whatever second. Effective intervention programs for both prima facie and test retardates will have to be addressed to the multiplicity of individual differences within socioeconomic and ethnic groups, as well as to the manifold differences between these groups.

References

Bandura, A., & Walters, R. H. *Social learning and personality development.* New York: Holt, Rinehart & Winston, 1963.

Baratz, J. C. A bi-dialectal task for determining language proficiency in economically disadvantaged Negro children. *Child Development,* 1969, **40,** 890-901.

Barnes, R. H. Behavioral changes caused by malnutrition in the rat and pig. In D. Glass (Ed.), *Environmental influences.* New York: Rockefeller University Press, 1968.

Bernard, J. S. *Marriage and family among Negroes.* Englewood Cliffs, N.J.: Prentice-Hall, 1966.

Bernstein, B. Social structure, language and learning. *Educational Research,* 1961, **3,** 163-176.

Biber, B. Premature structuring as a deterrent to creativity. *American Journal of Orthopsychiatry,* 1959, **29,** 280-290.

Bloom, B. S. *Stability and change in human characteristics.* New York: Wiley, 1964.

Canady, H. B. The effects of rapport on the IQ: A new approach to the problem of racial psychology. *Journal of Negro Education,* 1936, **5,** 209-219.

Cole, M., Gay, J., Glick, J. A., & Sharp, D. W. *The cultural context of learning and thinking.* New York: Basic Books, 1971.

Cravioto, J. Nutritional deficiencies and mental performance in childhood. In D. C. Glass (Ed.), *Biology and behavior: Environmental influences.* New York: Rockefeller University Press and Russell Sage Foundation, 1968.

Douvan, E. Social status and success strivings. *Journal of Abnormal and Social Psychology,* 1956, **52,** 219-223.

Elkind, D. Developmental studies of figurative perception. In L. Lipsitt & H. W. Reese (Eds.), *Recent advances in child development research.* New York: Academic Press, 1969.

Elkind, D. Teacher child contracts. *School Review,* 1971, **79,** 575-589.

Elkind, D. Cognitive growth cycles in mental development. In D. Katz (Ed.), *Nebraska symposium on motivation.* Lincoln: University of Nebraska Press, 1972.

Elkind, D., Deblinger, J., & Adler, D. Motivation and creativity: The context effect. *American Educational Research Association Journal,* 1970, **7,** 351-357.

Elkstein, R. *The challenge: Despair and hope in the conquest of human space; studies of the psychoanalytic treatment of severely disturbed children.* New York: Appleton-Century-Crofts, 1966.

Fleming, E. S., & Auttonen, R. G. Teacher expectancy as related to the academic and personal growth of primary age children. *Monographs of the Society for Research in Child Development,* 1971, **36,** 1-31.

Forrester, B. J., & Klaus, R. A. The effect of race of examiner on intelligence test scores of Negro kindergarten children. *Peabody Papers on Human Development,* 1964, **2,** 1-7.

Goodnow, J. Problems in research on culture and thought. In D. Elkind & J. H. Flavell (Eds.), *Studies in cognitive development.* New York: Oxford, 1969.

Greenfield, P. M. On culture and conservation. In J. S. Bruner, R. R. Olver, & P. Greenfield (Eds), *Studies in cognitive growth.* New York: Wiley, 1966.

Hernnstein, R. IQ. *The Atlantic,* 1971, **228,** 43-64 (September).

Hess, R. D., & Shipman, V. C. Early experience and the socialization of cognitive modes in children. *Child Development,* 1965, **36,** 869-886.

Jensen, A. R. How much can we boost IQ and scholastic achievement? *Harvard Educational Review,* 1969, **39,** 1-123.

Lennenberg, H. *Biological foundations of language.* New York: Wiley, 1967.

Long, E. The effect of programmed instruction in special skills during the preschool period on later ability patterns and academic achievement. *U.S. Office of Education Progress Report No. 1521.* Chapel Hill: University of North Carolina Press, 1966.

Lott, A. J., & Lott, B. E. *Negro and white youth.* New York: Holt, Rinehart & Winston, 1963.

Mussen, P., Urbano, P., & Boutourline-Young, H. Esplorazione del motivi per mezzo di un reattivo: II Classi sociali e motivazione fra adolescenti di origine Italiani. *Archivio de Psichologia, Neurologia e Psichiatria,* 1961, 22, 681-690.

Peluffo, N. Les notions de conservation et de causalite chez les enfants provenant de differents milieux physiques et socioculturels. *Archives de Psychologie,* 1962, 38, 75-90.

Rosenthal, R., & Jacobsen, L. Self-fulfilling prophecies in the classroom: Teachers' expectations as unintended determinants of intellectual competence. In M. Deutsch, I. Katz, & A. R. Jensen (Eds.), *Social class, race and psychological development.* New York: Holt, Rinehart & Winston, 1968.

Sigel, I. E., & Mermelstein, E. The effects of nonschooling on Piaget's conservation tasks. Paper presented at the meeting of the American Psychological Association, Chicago, 1965.

Stock, M. B., & Smyth, P. M. Does undernutrition during infancy inhibit brain growth and subsequent intellectual development? *Archives of Diseases in Childhood,* 1963, 38, 546-552.

Vernon, P. E. Environmental handicaps and intellectual development. *British Journal of Psychology,* 1965, 35, 1-12; 117-126.

Zigler, E., & Butterfield, E. C. Motivational aspects of changes in IQ test performance of culturally deprived nursery school children. *Child Development,* 1968, 39, 1-14.

Robert M. Allen and Barry J. Schwartz

Cognitive Development–A Means for Maturation and Measurement

COGNITIVE DEVELOPMENT may be viewed, measured, and even enhanced from many vantage points. This chapter describes a concept for achieving improvement in cognitive maturation, in its broadest sense, of residents of a state facility for the mentally retarded. However, the approach is not the usual academic one, but rather, the emphasis is on the variables significant in the activities of daily living. Certainly this approach may well be considered a phase in the total cognitive development of the retarded child. Its core is the divisional concept.

The usual organization of a residential facility for the retarded—a department-centered and profession-centered structure—is seen in figure 1. This traditional, vertical mode of organization was replaced by four divisions, each with a specialized program and team of professional and paraprofessional personnel for serving and instructing the residents.

The implementation of the divisional concept was facilitated by a Hospital Improvement Program Grant from HEW

Robert M. Allen, Ph.D., is professor of psychology in the Department of Psychology and Pediatrics, University of Miami.

Barry J. Schwartz is a graduate student in psychology at the University of Miami.

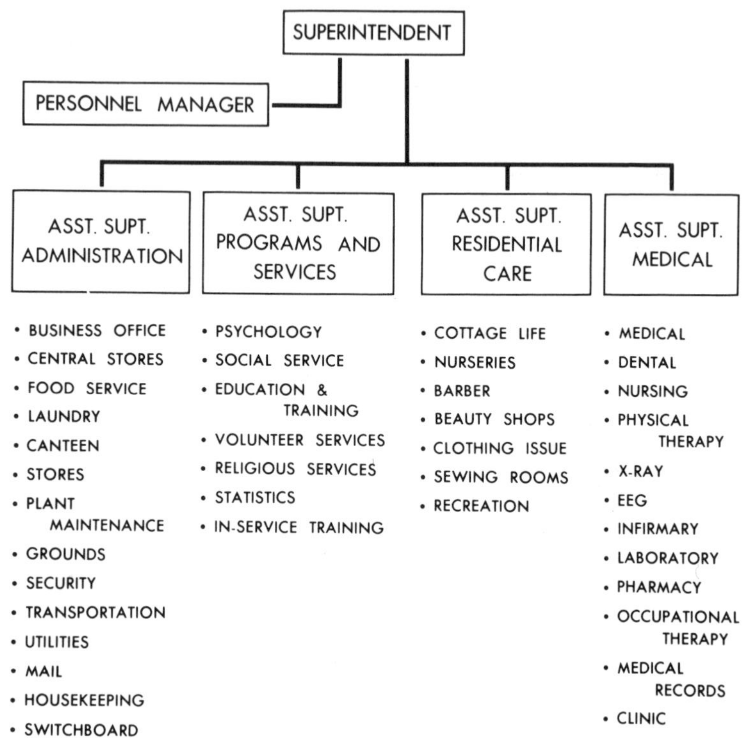

Figure 1. The traditional vertical organizational structure of a residential facility for the mentally retarded.

Social and Rehabilitation Services entitled, "Intensive Programming for Optimal Resident Development."[1] Of the six major goals of the project this chapter deals with two objectives: (a) to measure the effects of intensive specialized treatment programs on the cognitive growth and development of the retarded residents, and (b) to compare empirically the effectiveness of the four-divisional approach to the single, large, multipurpose facility and to give the results to date. This divisional model is offered to administrators as one effective way for managing the large multipurpose institution. One striking advantage of this model that will be-

1. Hospital Improvement Program Grant (HIP) No. 1-R20 02149-01.

come apparent to administrators is that the resident is always the "center of things" and that the emphasis of all employees is on programming.

L. Dunn (1969) contends that a century of failure of the large, multipurpose residential facilities is long enough; the effectiveness of other approaches needs to be tested. He proposes that the efficacy of small, special-purpose facilities be examined as one alternative. The obstacles and problems that minimized the effectiveness of the programs and services at Sunland Training Center (STC) in Miami were largely a result of the adopted concepts of operation. These concepts, including the organizational structure and procedures, were taken from large multipurpose residential facilities, which were based on the procedures of the decades from 1850 to 1890 rather than on the methods of the present that concentrate planning and action on behalf of the retarded.

A New Approach

To ameliorate the shortcomings of the traditional organizational structure, Miami Sunland Training Center had to move away from this outmoded concept. It would be impossible to plan and to implement modern, meaningful programs and bind them to an antiquated model. An ad hoc study committee proposed that if Miami STC were to become an effective facility its present departmental or vertical structure would have to be changed into at least four separate, but interrelated, basic divisional and intensive specialized treatment programs to meet the needs of the residents. The organizational structure of the major departments and various disciplines, such as social work, psychology, education, recreation, nursing, and cottage life, had to be broken down and blended into meaningful interdisciplinary divisional teams, one team to work completely in each division. Each division was headed by a program director. The various professional team members were responsible for their respective division programs rather than to a specific

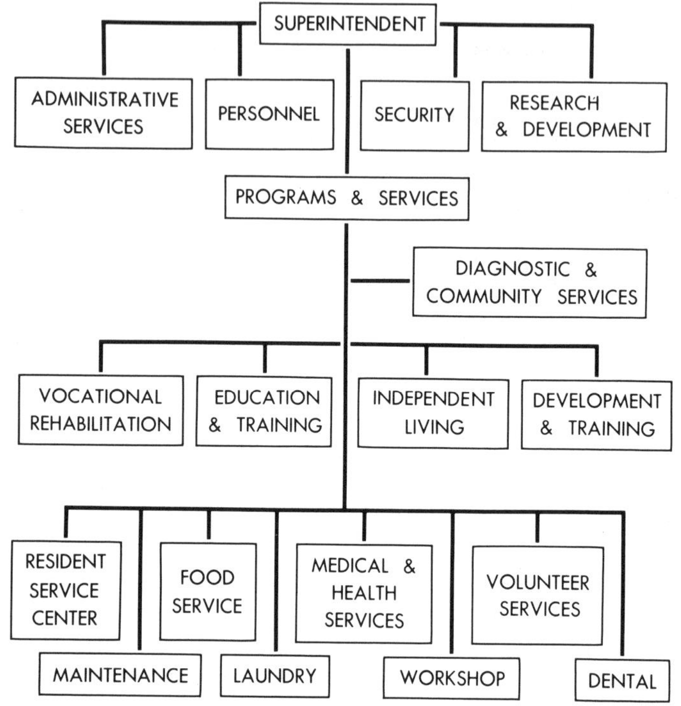

Figure 2. The divisional or horizontal organization of a residential facility for the mentally retarded.

department (see figure 2). Thus, in terms of meeting the program needs of all residents, the horizontal organizational structure would replace the vertical one. In reality the large multipurpose institution became a number of highly specialized institutions.

The Four Divisions

Each of the four divisions (Cortazzo & Allen, 1971) has an interdisciplinary team consisting of the program director, psychologist, physician, social worker, cottage group shift supervisor, cottage parents and supervisors, recreation therapists, nurse, cottage training instructors, food service work-

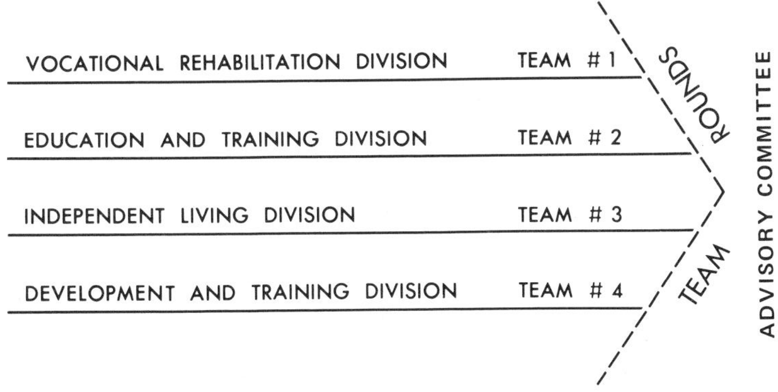

Figure 3. The advisory teams constituting the advisory committee.

ers, in-service training instructors, and other related staff. An advisory team circulates on a "team round" basis to all four divisions, as in figure 3. The advisory team is made up of the directors of the former major departments of cottage life, psychology, social service, recreation, and medical. It evaluates the progress in the implementation of the divisional concepts, acts as a sounding board for proposals and ideas, acts as a consultant when needed in program areas, and aids in solving problems. In addition to making rounds of each division, the advisory team meets quarterly with all four divisional teams, along with the superintendent, business officer, plant superintendent, and other key personnel. The purpose of these meetings is to discuss the overall status of the institution, especially as it relates to the stated goals and specific objectives of each division.

Theoretically, there are many intermediary program planes between divisions so that as residents grow and develop in a program plane horizontally they reach a level for moving up or down vertically into other planes or another division appropriate for their needs. Vertical movement is utilized also for given periods of time for specific evaluations of residents.

Regardless of the division residents are in, they receive the same amount of attention and emphasis in their programs, although the programs may be different in content as deemed necessary. The principles underlying the divisional concept are: (1) every resident is programmed, (2) programming is made meaningful and coordinated over a 24-hour period for settings both in the cottage and outside the cottage, (3) programming is comprehensive in nature since the program decisions for a child are team prescriptions carried out by assigned team members in reasonable harmony, (4) the residents and programs receive more frequent evaluations, and (5) parents of residents are becoming more involved in group and individual meetings. The divisional concept represents considerable development of training principles for programming within the cottages, especially in the Development and Training division, as well as for the other three divisions.

Development and Training Division

The Development and Training Division is for residents of all ages who are profoundly retarded, level -5, and still need to learn the very rudimentary activities of daily living, such as toilet training and self-feeding.

A wide variety of behavior-shaping techniques have been developed encompassing the following: (1) self-feeding programs; (2) toilet training; (3) self-dressing; (4) purposeful self-locomotion; (5) communication (learning commands, gestures, making needs known, and elementary language); (6) brushing teeth; (7) clusters of appropriate behavior activities upon arising; (8) clusters of behavior activities around mealtime and self-feeding; (9) clusters of behavior activities around bedtime, toileting, bathing, and brushing teeth; and (10) recreational and simple occupational activities.

Independent Living Division

This division is designed for residents who are at least sixteen years old and who do not seem to have the potential for competitive employment. With proper programs they can, however, become sheltered employees either in a community workshop or in an institution. Most of these individuals have been trained to have the potential for caring completely for their own self-help needs, such as dressing, feeding, and toileting, and can get by with a minimal to medium amount of supervision in most daily living activities. Many will return to the community later and live in a community group-living house for five or six retarded persons and work in a sheltered workshop or in an institution under supervision. This division has different training units to meet the diversified program needs and behavior of the residents. The five phases in this program are: (1) training in improving independent personal skills and personal adjustment; (2) training in useful cottage skills and cottage peer adjustment; (3) training in work skills and work adjustment; (4) training in community skills and community living adjustment; and (5) reevaluation, placement, and follow-up guidance.

Education and Training Division

The Education and Training Division serves residents up to sixteen years of age who have the ability or potential to acquire through education and training those educational, personal, communicational, social, occupational, and vocational skills that will lead to independence or semi-independence in adulthood. The units in this division include preschool (three to seven years), primary (eight to twelve years), intermediate (ten to thirteen years), and secondary (thirteen to sixteen years) residents. This division emphasizes the development and use of language and motor skills in the tool subjects, social competency, occupational information, prevocational training, home economics, vocational guidance, and some in-school work experience. If residents are still in the institution beyond the age of sixteen, they can continue in this division, or, if necessary, be moved either to the Independent Living or Vocational Rehabilitation Divisions, depending on their program needs.

Vocational Rehabilitation Division

To be eligible for the Vocational Rehabilitation Division, residents must be at least sixteen years old and have the potential for competitive employment in the community. They must be able to completely take care of their personal needs and clean and maintain their rooms or cottages. There are two sections in this division. One is an intensive adjustment section for residents who have serious personal or social adjustment problems; the second is for those with acceptable personal and social skills. Included in this division are four half-way houses located on campus. The phases in the program are: (1) vocational and psychological evaluations of clients; (2) individual resident rehabilitation plans; (3) rehabilitation counseling; (4) vocational and community orientation; (5) initial on-campus vocational training; (6) intensive on-campus work training; (7) community work training and employment; and (8) community placement and training.

Evaluation of the Project

An effort has been made to determine the effect of the divisional concept programs on the growth and development of the residents. In this evaluation the residents have served as their own controls. The degree of improvement is derived from score differences between the first and second evaluations of each resident taken one year apart. The evaluations were made with a modified version of the Adaptive Behavior Check List (ABCL). (Since the second reevaluation a revised ABCL with sixty items has been devised.) Moreover, control groups in two similar multipurpose institutions—Fort Myers and Marianna Sunland Training Center—were similarly evaluated. The ABCL comparisons were also made between the four Miami Sunland Training Center divisions and four hypothetically established divisions in the control groups from the two institutions mentioned.

Method

In August 1969 each resident at Miami Sunland Training Center was assigned to one of the four program divisions on the basis of recommendations by the cottage parents and supervisors. Each division had special programs designed to benefit its particular residents.

The proportion of residents in each division was approximately 15 percent in vocational rehabilitation, 35 percent in both education and training and independent living, and 15 percent in development and training. For each division the means and ranges for IQ and chronological age (CA) were obtained. On the basis of these values, a stratified random sample of 400 subjects (*S*s) was selected from two other state Sunland Training Centers, 200 from the Sunland Training Center at Fort Myers, and 200 from the Sunland Training Center at Marianna, the control groups. The IQs and CAs are presented in table 1. Throughout the analyses

Table 1. Mean IQ and CA (in months) of the *S*s of the three Sunland Training Centers, by assigned divisions

	Miami		Fort Myers		Marianna	
Divisions	IQ	CA	IQ	CA	IQ	CA
All *S*s	40.7	251.5	34.0	223.4	33.2	220.6
Vocational Rehabilitation	57.7	313.2	59.3	271.7	55.1	250.6
Education and Training	42.0	153.3	28.4	149.6	32.0	147.7
Independent Living	40.5	344.4	35.3	273.8	31.8	284.4
Development and Training	25.1	221.2	19.4	231.4	17.4	212.7

of the data, means are given for each division separately and for all residents combined.

Following divisional assignment, the rating of the ABCL was completed for the Miami residents. The checklist was also filled in for the 400 residents by the appropriate personnel in the two control Sunland Training Centers. During the year following the first rating, the residents at Miami Sunland Training Center were exposed to the programs and services of their respective divisions (the experimental population). The residents in the two other Sunland Training

Centers continued to function within the traditional concept of institutional organization, taking advantage of all programs normally provided. *It is important to note that the three institutions are staffed in a proportionately equal manner, i.e., the staff-to-resident ratio is similar for all State of Florida Sunland Training Centers.* The Hospital Improvement Program Grant provided no additional funds for extra cottage personnel. The *organization* of the personnel and programs rather than the sheer number of staff members serves as the independent variable.

One year later a second assessment with the ABCL was accomplished for the study populations in the three STCs. Miami obtained second evaluations for 666 of the 674 residents initially rated, Fort Myers reevaluated 190 of the original 200, and Marianna rerated 182 of the original 200 *S*s. The data are based only on those *S*s for whom both first and second evaluations could be obtained. In all cases ratings on the ABCL were made by cottage parents, and where possible the second evaluator was the same individual who made the first rating.

The ABCL consists of seventy-two items, each of which provides three possible ratings. Three points were awarded for behavior indicative of the highest level of adaptive behavior, two points for behavior of some lesser adaptive value, and one point for the poorest adaptation. (The revised sixty-item ABCL is appended to the end of this chapter. The original ABCL's seventy-two items factored down to these final sixty items.)

Details of the checklist items are available elsewhere (Allen, Cortazzo, & Adamo, 1970). However, a factor analysis discloses that the ABCL encompasses three functional areas of adaptation: (1) the *basic* functions, which include items 1 to 30 concerning such daily elemental functions as eating, dressing, and toileting; (2) the *primary* functions, items 31 to 46, covering communication skills, namely, following instructions, speech patterns, etc.; and (3) the *secondary* functions, items 47 to 72, describing social skills, sharing with others, responsibility, and perseverance. Each assessment with the checklist yielded four scores: (1) total score, the sum for all seventy-two items, ranging from 72 to 216; (2) basic score, varying between 30 and 90 points for the thirty items; (3) primary score, the sum for the sixteen items, varying between 16 and 48 points; and (4) secondary score, consisting of from 26 to 78 points for the twenty-six items. (The new sixty-item functions are: basic functions, items 1 to 19, 57 points maximum; primary functions, items 20 to 34; 45 points maximum; and secondary functions, items 35 to 60, 78 points maximum for a maximum total of 180 points.)

In attempting to provide control populations of approximately equivalent age and intelligence to each other and to the experimental group, we used the technique of stratified random sampling. After the results from the second evaluation were collected, the control *S*s were assigned to one of the four divisions in the same proportion as the *S*s in the Miami divisions. As previously stated, the assignment of control *S*s to each division was based on IQ and CA criteria. Divisional assignments were hypothetical since neither control STC was organized to function within the divisional concept.

Despite attempts to match the *S*s in the three institutions, complete success was not attained. We might remember that equality of human subjects for *all* parameters is a nonobtainable desideratum even within the laboratory. In this study we are dealing with the problems of retardates in institutions *"au naturel."* The differences among the STCs may be seen in table 1. For example, for all *S*, analysis of variance indicated that the Miami sample has a significantly ($p < 0.01$) higher mean IQ than either of the samples from Fort Myers or Marianna. The mean CA of the Independent Living Division at Miami is higher than at the control institutions. Similar differences exist in the other divisions. A possible explanation may be that all residents at Miami were involved in this study whereas only 200 *S*s were chosen from their respective populations in each of the control STCs. Even though these control populations were stratified according to CA and IQ criteria, a tendency may have been to exclude the very old and the very bright residents from the study groups. As a precaution against making unfair equations of samples with varying CA and IQ characteristics, no direct comparisons of the three STCs will be made; instead, the progress of each STC population will be assessed independently.

Results and Discussion

As previously mentioned, the results are analyzed in terms of whether or not there is a significant change in ABCL scores within each of the three institutions. Analysis of variance is used exclusively. All four dependent measures (ABCL total, basic, primary, and secondary scores) are examined, and the *S*s are viewed both from within their divisions and across all divisions.

Figure 4 presents the means of all *S*s in each STC in the study. Figure 4A discloses that the *S*s of the three institutions increased their ABCL total scores over the year of the study. Analysis of variance for each center specifies that the three populations improved significantly ($p < 0.01$). This change is to be expected because the subjects have had one more year of experience in learning how to cope with living. Finding a small but significant positive correlation of age with ABCL total score would also indicate adaptive improvement over time.

The groups also show a significant increase in their basic scores from first to second rating (see figure 4B). Fort Myers and Miami *S*s improved moderately whereas the Marianna sample showed a significant mean increase of almost four points. This improvement is the result of an intensive program in self-help skills in progress during the year between the first and second evaluations. The dramatic betterment by this control population is quite impressive, but at the same time there are drawbacks. The Marianna *S*s failed to show significant increases in the primary and secondary ABCL scores; figure 4C shows a small drop in score for the primary measure.

Miami *S*s showed significant ($p < 0.01$) improvement for

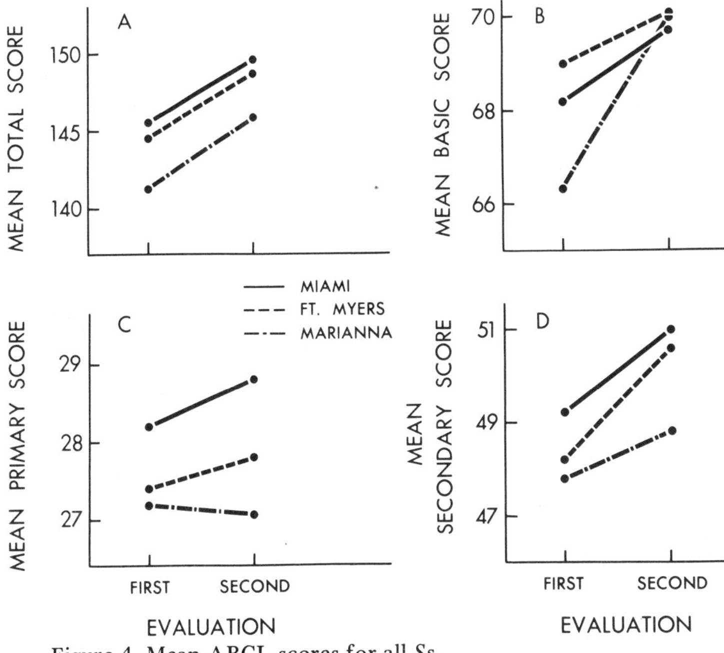

Figure 4. Mean ABCL scores for all *S*s.

both the primary and secondary scores (figures 4C and 4D). The Fort Myers group progressed significantly in the secondary score, but not in the primary. Thus, Miami *S*s improved in the three functional areas, Fort Myers *S*s in two areas, and the Marianna sample in only one area. These findings suggest that the Miami *S*s had a more balanced program that included a broad spectrum of teaching and learning adaptation experiences. The divisional concept provides programs and services that result in actual, and potential for, improvement in the three functioning areas rather than in just basic activities of daily living. The effects of this broad program are further illustrated in the data for each separate division.

Vocational Rehabilitation Division

From figure 5A we may see that only the Miami group showed significant ($p < 0.05$) gain in the total score for the

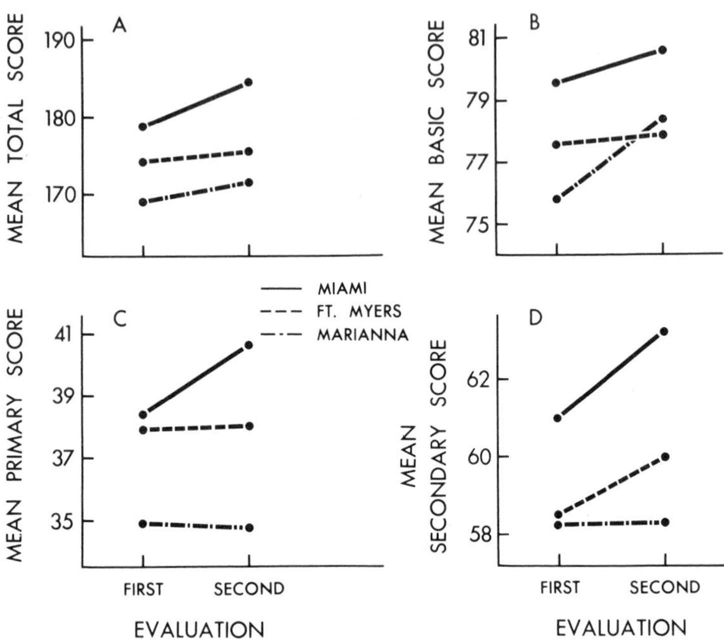

Figure 5. Mean ABCL scores for *S*s in the Vocational Rehabilitation Division.

*S*s in this division. This is important since these *S*s have the best potential for leaving the institution. Their having the highest IQs (see table 1) may result in a ceiling ABCL score beyond which the checklist does not discriminate. Within the traditionally organized institution, special programs for training residents of this caliber are usually the exception. The residents therefore may progress to a certain level (via the standard programs) and go no further because the programs are designed primarily for those with lesser capacities. Another variable leading to stagnation among these residents is that their general good behavior causes no real problems for cottage parents and results in a "let well enough alone" attitude. The divisional structure provides programs aimed at just this type of resident.

Figure 5 presents means of four dependent measures for the *S*s of the Vocational Rehabilitation Division only. The results justify the implementation of a specific type of program. Since basic scores are so high for these *S*s (80 of 90 possible points), further training in this area is probably not pressing and emphasis on the primary and secondary skills would be a better investment. B. J. Schwartz and A. E. Couture (1972) also reached this conclusion. The seeming lack of a noticeable increase of the mean basic scores from the first to second assessments for the Miami *S*s is expected because of the significant increases in both primary ($p < 0.01$) and secondary ($p < 0.06$) scores (figures 5C and 5D).

Fort Myers *S*s do not show significant improvements in any of the ABCL functional areas although the trend for the secondary area (figure 5D) is in the upward direction. Marianna *S*s achieved significant ($p < 0.06$) growth on the basic score, figure 5B, undoubtedly as a result of the center's intensive program. The data in figures 5C and 5D suggest that this emphasis may be unduly restrictive for these *S*s inasmuch as there is no observable gain in either the primary or secondary functions, where improvement is more directly related to possible community living. The growth in performance reflected by the basic score is not to be dismissed, however, for it is certainly indicative of an excellent program of training in the essential elements of daily life. Moreover, having reached this level of success with basic activities, the *S*s are probably ready for experiences in primary and perhaps secondary functions. The divisional organization for the delivery of programs and services to the Miami residents appears to be providing such experiences for the vocational rehabilitation population.

Education and Training Division

The distinctive personal feature of the *S*s in this division is their age. As a group they are the youngest residents. Their mean IQs place them in the -3 and -4 levels. Because of their youth, these residents should be able to make a great deal of progress since their behavior is more malleable than that of the older residents.

Figure 6 presents the scores for the four dependent measures for the first and second evaluations. Figure 6A, total

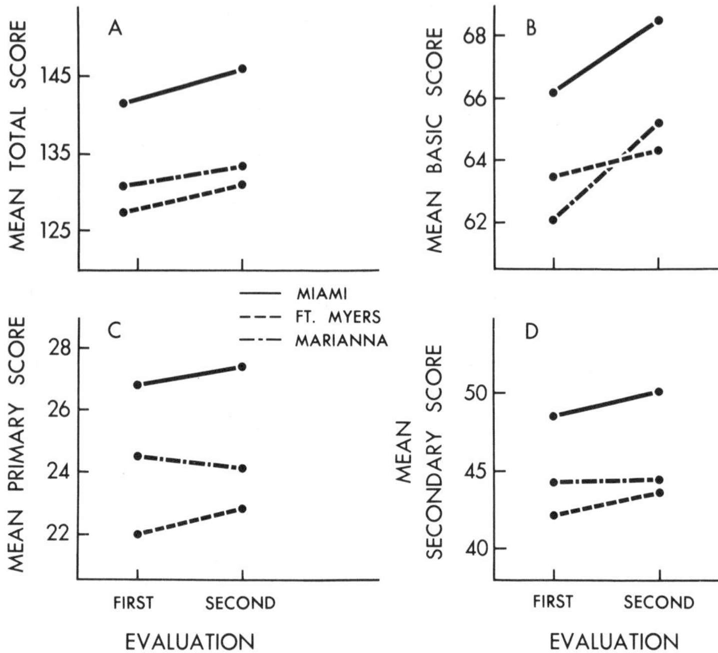

Figure 6. Mean ABCL scores for *S*s in the Education and Training Division.

scores, indicates that the *S*s in the three institutions do show progress in the growth direction. The Miami *S*s' growth approaches significance ($p < 0.10$), but Marianna's slight gain is not significant.

The basic scores in figure 6B disclose the influence of the intensive self-care program at Marianna. These *S*s improved significantly ($p < 0.01$) on basic items from the first to second evaluation. The other functional areas (figure 6C and 6D) show no increase and even a slight drop for the Marianna *S*s. The increase in the basic skills for the Miami education and training population is highly significant ($p < 0.01$). In addition, the Miami group evidences movement in the upward direction in both the primary and secondary scores, although only the secondary score approaches significance ($p < 0.06$). The Fort Myers group made modest improvement in all three functional areas. None of these gains was significant when the data were subjected to an analysis of variance.

One important aspect for progress in training STC residents such as those in the Education and Training Division is to utilize the self-help skills they have acquired, which are evaluated by the basic items of the ABCL. The divisional concept is geared to provide programs that involve training in these skills. It seems, too, that the self-help programs at the Marianna Sunland Training Center are quite advantageous for its residents.

The improvement by the Miami *S*s in the three functional areas measured by the ABCL supports the balanced program provided through the divisional mode of delivering programs and services to these retardates.

Independent Living Division

As with the Education and Training Division, age is the unique characteristic of the *S*s in the Independent Living Division. The education and training *S*s are seventeen years of age and younger; the independent living residents are all over seventeen. Table 1 presents the mean age and IQ of the independent living residents in the three STCs. The control *S*s from both Fort Myers and Marianna STCs are about four or five years younger than the Miami independent living residents. Analysis of variance proves this difference to be significant at the $p < 0.01$ level. Since they are younger, these *S*s may have had more potential for improvement, thus making a direct comparison with the Miami group difficult to support.

The three institutions exhibited significant total score improvements from the first to second evaluation ($p < 0.01$ for Fort Myers and Marianna; $p < 0.05$ for Miami). Figure 7A graphically presents these advances. The steeper slopes for the control institution *S*s indicate that they made greater progress than the Miami group. Such a difference may be the result of the age differences.

The significant ($p < 0.01$) improvement on the basic items by both the Fort Myers and Marianna sample populations may be seen in Figure 7B. The lack of forward progress by

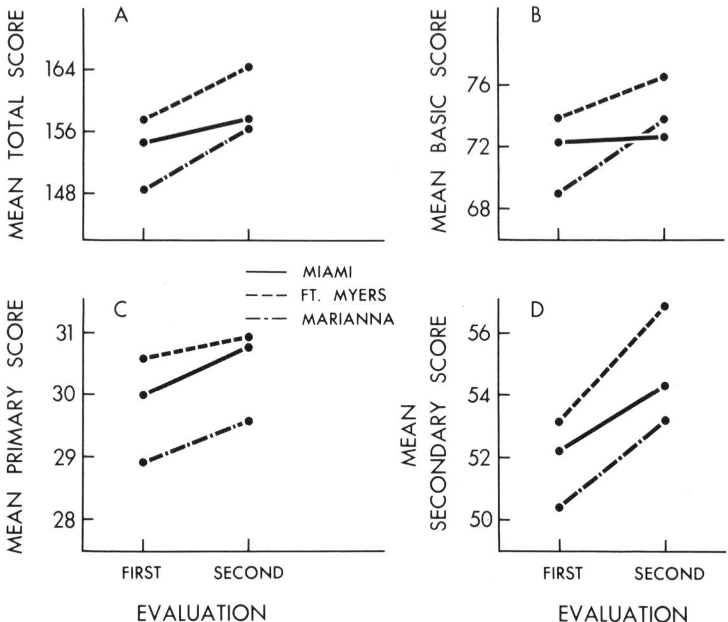

Figure 7. Mean ABCL scores for *S*s in the Independent Living Division.

the Miami *S*s may again have been due to the older age of Miami's independent living residents and their more entrenched personal habits.

Figures 7C and 7D disclose the changes in primary and secondary scores. The Miami group improved significantly in both scores ($p < 0.05$ for primary and $p < 0.01$ for secondary) although the controls failed to show significant increase on the primary score. The special divisional program for Miami's independent living residents emphasizes these two functional areas; this emphasis is reflected in the higher scores. Both control groups, however, attained significantly better scores on reevaluation for the secondary functions. These data suggest that *S*s may be more amenable to learning social behavior than communication skills assessed by the primary portion of the ABCL. The significant gain by Miami *S*s in the primary score suggests that perhaps with proper programming and intensive exposure to appropriate experiences these residents did make advances in communication skills.

Development and Training Division

As may be seen in table 1, the residents of the Development and Training Division have the lowest mean IQ of the four divisions. The vast majority of the *S*s in this division are at the -4 and -5 levels. They constitute the custodial cases in most institutions and need almost constant attention and assistance. Many of these residents require help in dressing and eating and some with toileting.

Because of the time and care these residents require, it is almost imperative to focus on improving their self-care skills. Since the *basic* function items measure just such skills, an increase in the score for development and training

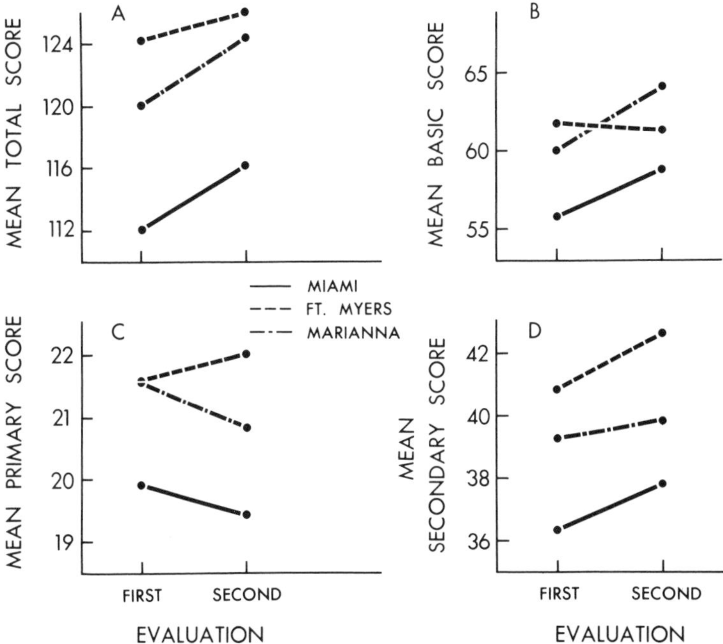

Figure 8. Mean ABCL scores for *S*s in the Development and Training Division.

residents is important. Figure 8 shows that both Miami and Marianna STC groups increased significantly at the $p<0.01$ and $p<0.05$ levels, respectively, from first to second evaluations. Evidently, the intensive program at Marianna is functionally relevant and may be credited for the improvement assessed by the basic items. The data seem to reflect a similarity in the basic training program objectives at Miami and Marianna STCs.

Among the development and training residents, there is room for a great deal of progress in basic functions. Until these residents achieve sufficient skills, it may be necessary to be less demanding of the primary and secondary functions. The relatively lower basic score by the Fort Myers sample is puzzling and disturbing–puzzling in the sense that some improvement in basic functions usually comes about with the passage of time alone, and disturbing because residents earning such low ratings cannot afford to deteriorate.

Fort Myers *S*s do exhibit growth trends in both primary and secondary scores. Such increments, however, proved to be not statistically significant. The declines in primary scores shown by both the Miami and Marianna samples were not significant, nor were the modes increments in secondary scores.

Since the basic functional area is of considerable importance for these *S*s, programs for them should deal with these items. Yet the Fort Myers *S*s have shown that these residents can move upward in both primary and secondary functioning. It would seem that with an ideal program such residents should be able to move forward in all three functional areas, a feat that none of these three STCs has executed successfully.

Conclusion

This two-year study shows that as a group the mentally retarded in state institutions do learn with the passage of time and exposure to experiences. The real question is whether this progress may be enhanced by means of one mode or a combination of modes for delivering programs and services to the retardate.

The point to this study is the greater effectiveness of the traditional (or vertical) versus the divisional (or horizontal) organizational structure for such delivery. The philosophy seems to favor the latter approach. The findings of this investigation also support the divisional concept as a generally more efficient framework within which personal, social, and real or potential vocational progress may be expected. Equally significant is the collateral finding that the cottage personnel reacted favorably to this model for improved programming and service for the Miami Sunland Training Center resident (Allen, Cortazzo, & Schwartz, 1972).

References

Allen, R. M., & Cortazzo, A. D. *Psychosocial and educational aspects and problems of mental retardation.* Springfield, Ill.: Charles C Thomas, 1970.

Allen, R. M., Cortazzo, A. D., & Adamo, C. C. Factors in an adaptive behavior check list for use with retardates. *Training School Bulletin,* 1970, **67**, 144-157.

Allen, R. M., Cortazzo, A. D., & Schwartz, B. J. Attitudinal survey of a hospital improvement project at work. *Mental Retardation,* in press.

Allen, R. M., Cortazzo, A. D., & Toister, R. P. *The role of genetics in mental retardation.* Coral Gables, Fla.: University of Miami Press, 1971.

Cortazzo, A. D., & Allen, R. M. The divisional approach to achieving hospital improvement goals. *Training School Bulletin,* 1971, **61**, 235-243.

Cortazzo, A. D., & Foshee, J. G. Intensive programming for optimal resident development. *Mental Retardation,* 1970, **8** (6).

Cortazzo, A. D., Schwartz, B. J., & Allen, R. M. *The divisional concept: a residential model to intensive programming for optimal resident development.* Miami, Fla.: Southern Foundation for Mentally Retarded Children, 1972.

Dunn, L. Small, special-purpose residential facilities for the retarded. In R. B. Kugel & W. P. Wolfenberger (Eds.), *Changing patterns in residential services for the mentally retarded.* Washington, D.C.: U.S. Government Printing Office, 1969.

Dybwad, G. Action implications. In R. B. Kugel & W. P.

Wolfensberger (Eds.), *Changing patterns in residential services for the mentally retarded.* Washington, D.C.: U.S. Government Printing Office, 1969.

Kugel, R. B. Why innovative action? In R. B. Kugel and W. P. Wolfensberger (Eds.), *Changing patterns in residential services for the mentally retarded.* Washington, D.C.: U.S. Government Printing Office, 1969.

National Association for Retarded Children. *A needed next step in implementing the federal role in improving residential care of the retarded.* New York: Author, 1968.

PCMR Message (President's Committee on Mental Retardation), Washington, D.C., U.S. Government Printing Office, 1967.

Schwartz, B. J., & Couture, A. E. A statistical confirmation of the divisional approach. *Training School Bulletin,* 1972, **69**, 25-30.

Appendix

ADAPTIVE BEHAVIOR CHECK LIST (1972 Revision)

The attached check list[1] consists of a number of statements that describe some of the ways children act in different situations. Please select only the one statement that best describes the individual. Rate every item.

NAME OF RESIDENT:..

RATER: ....

COTTAGE:...

DATE:...

Part I: BASIC FUNCTIONS

1. EATING: Select the *one statement* that best describes the person's ability to eat.

..... 3. Able to eat independently.

..... 2. Able to eat with some help.

..... 1. Must be fed.

---

1. Adaptive Behavior Check List prepared by the Adaptive Behavior Project, Parsons State Hospital and Training Center.
NIMH Grant Number 5-R11 MH 14901

2. USE OF TABLE UTENSILS: Select the *one statement* that best describes the person's use of table utensils.

   ..... 3. Uses knife, fork, and spoon correctly and fairly neatly while eating.

   ..... 2. Feeds self with utensils but with some spilling or other accidents.

   ..... 1. Uses fingers in eating.

3. DRINKING: Select the *one statement* that best describes the person's ability to drink from a cup or glass.

   ..... 3. Drinks without spilling, holding glass or cup in one hand.

   ..... 2. Drinks from cup or glass unassisted—considerable spilling.

   ..... 1. Does not drink from cup or glass unassisted.

4. TABLE MANNERS: Select the *one statement* that best describes the person's use of table manners.

   ..... 3. Chews and swallows food properly.

   ..... 2. Chews and swallows but drops food and is otherwise not a neat eater.

   ..... 1. Eating habits are entirely unacceptable—spills food, talks with food in mouth, eats too fast, and plays with food.

5. TOILET TRAINING: Select the *one statement* that best describes the person's level of toilet training.

   ..... 3. Never has toilet accidents.

   ..... 2. Occasionally has toilet accidents during the day.

   ..... 1. Frequently has toilet accidents during the day; i.e., not toilet trained.

6. ACCEPTABLE MODE OF CLOTHING: Select the *one statement* that best describes the person's mode of clothing.

   ..... 3. Clothes are as neat and clean as possible and worn appropriately.

   ..... 2. Wears soiled clothing; has to be reminded to put on clean clothing.

   ..... 1. Totally disinterested in clothes and has to be supervised if clean clothes are to be worn.

7. CARES FOR SELF AT TOILET: Select the *one statement* that best describes the person's level of care for self at toilet.

..... 3. Wipes self, flushes toilet, and washes self properly.

..... 2. Needs help in toileting and washing.

..... 1. Has to be put on toilet seat, wiped by attendant, and washed. Unable to care for himself at toilet.

8. WASHES HANDS AND FACE IN AN ACCEPTABLE WAY: Select the *one statement* that best describes the person's level of washing.

..... 3. Washes hands and face with soap.

..... 2. Washes hands and face with water with help.

..... 1. Does not wash hands and face; has to be washed.

9. PREPARES AND TAKES BATH OR SHOWER UNAIDED: Select *one statement* that best describes the person's level of bathing.

..... 3. Bathes self and dries self alone.

..... 2. Attempts to bathe self, but needs supervision.

..... 1. Does not cooperate in taking a bath or shower.

10. KEEPS SELF CLEAN WITHOUT BEING REMINDED: Select the *one statement* that best describes the person's level of keeping self clean.

..... 3. Changes underwear regularly and tries to be clean.

..... 2. Is neat and clean, but only with attendant's supervision.

..... 1. Does not make an effort to be clean.

11. BRUSHES TEETH: Select the *one statement* that best describes the person's ability to brush his teeth.

..... 3. Applies toothpaste and brushes with up-and-down motions.

..... 2. Brushes teeth with supervision.

..... 1. Makes no attempt to brush teeth.

12. ACCEPTABLY GROOMED: Select the *one statement* that best describes the acceptability of person's hair style and use of makeup.

..... 3. Combs or brushes hair well; is clean shaven, or makeup is presentable.

..... 2. Uses too much makeup or puts it on incorrectly, (man—improper use of hair oil, cologne) or does not shave often enough (woman—fails to shave legs or underarms often enough).

..... 1. Unshaven, unkempt, sloppy about grooming self.

13. DRESSES SELF WITHOUT ASSISTANCE: Select the *one statement* that best describes the person's dressing ability.

..... 3. Buttons or zips dress, shirt, pants, or shirt without assistance.

..... 2. Dresses self with assistance.

..... 1. Does not cooperate in dressing by extending arms or legs and needs almost complete help in dressing.

14. UNDRESSES SELF AT NIGHT OR WHEN BATHING WITHOUT ASSISTANCE: Select the *one statement* that best describes the person's undressing ability.

..... 3. Unbuttons or unzips dress, shirt, pants, or skirt without assistance.

..... 2. Needs some help in undressing.

..... 1. Does not cooperate in undressing by extending arms or legs and needs considerable help.

15. PUTS ON AND REMOVES SHOES WITHOUT ASSISTANCE: Select the *one statement* that best describes the person's ability to put on and remove shoes.

..... 3. Can put on and take off shoes correctly and ties and unties laces without assistance.

..... 2. Can tie and untie laces with assistance. Able to put on and remove shoes.

..... 1. Does not remove shoes without assistance.

16. MISCELLANEOUS INDEPENDENT FUNCTIONING: Select the *one statement* that best describes the person.

..... 3. Can manage activities of daily living (everyday functions as a human being) with a minimal amount of supervision—fairly independent.

..... 2. Needs direction and/or supervision but can get through the day fairly well.

..... 1. Is completely dependent and almost purely custodial.

17. WALKING: Select the *one statement* that best describes the person's ability to walk.

..... 3. Can walk and go up and down stairs alone.

..... 2. Can walk alone but needs help on stairs.

..... 1. Cannot walk without some kind of support or help.

18. POSTURE WHEN WALKING, SITTING, AND STANDING: Select the *one statement* that best describes the person's posture.

..... 3. Walks reasonably well, picking up feet, head up to see where he (or she) is going, gait is satisfactory.

..... 2. Walks in a slow, unevenly balanced manner, with head down and/or mouth open.

..... 1. Shuffles, spreads feet, posture very poor thus interfering with good walking technique.

19. ACCURACY: Select the *one statement* that best describes the person's accuracy.

..... 3. Deliberate and accurate.

..... 2. Inaccurate but recognizes errors.

..... 1. Seems to have no controlled movement.

Part II: PRIMARY FUNCTIONS

20. EATING IN PUBLIC: Select the *one statement* that you feel would best describe the person's ability to use public eating facilities.

..... 3. Orders complete meals in restaurants.

..... 2. Orders simple meals like hamburgers or hot dogs and soft drinks at the Canteen.

..... 1. Could not use public facilities at all.

21. TELLING TIME: Select the *one statement* that best describes the person's understanding of time.

..... 3. Can tell time by clock or watch correctly.

..... 2. Is capable of stating the correct time by the hour and/or half hour.

..... 1. Does not tell time.

22. GENERAL TIME CONCEPT: Select the *one statement* that best describes the person's time concept.

..... 3. Names and understands the days of the week; e.g., Monday, Tuesday, etc.

..... 2. Refers correctly to morning and afternoon but does not name days.

..... 1. Cannot relate time of day or days of week.

23. ERRANDS: Select the *one statement* that best describes the person's ability to run errands.

..... 3. Can go to several shops and specify different items.

..... 2. Can be sent on an errand for simple purchasing with a note.

..... 1. Cannot be sent on errands.

24. PURCHASING: Select the *one statement* that best describes the person's ability to make his own purchases.

..... 3. Selects own clothing and accessories.

..... 2. Does shopping with supervision.

..... 1. Does no shopping.

25. WRITING: Select the *one statement* that best describes the person's ability to write.

..... 3. Writes or prints short notes.

..... 2. Writes or prints own name only.

..... 1. Cannot write or print any words.

26. ABILITY TO SAY AT LEAST A FEW WORDS: Select the *one statement* that best describes the person's ability to say a few words.

..... 3. Can make wants known in acceptable speech.

..... 2. Indicates needs with single words or short phrases.

..... 1. Unable to speak sufficiently to communicate needs and wants.

27. GENERALLY CLEAR AND UNDERSTANDABLE SPEECH: Select the *one statement* that best describes the person's ability to speak clearly.

..... 3. Speech is comprehensible.

..... 2. Speech is difficult to understand.

..... 1. No speech.

28. SENTENCE STRUCTURE: Select the *one statement* that best describes the sentences used by the person.

..... 3. Sometimes uses complex sentences containing "because," and "but," and asks questions using such words as why, how, what, etc.

..... 2. Speaks in simple sentences of three words or not at all.

..... 1. Speaks either in incomplete sentences or not at all.

29. VOCABULARY: Select the *one statement* that best describes the person's vocabulary.

..... 3. Talks about action, people, or objects when describing pictures.

..... 2. Asks for at least ten things by their names.

..... 1. Is nearly nonverbal.

30. READING: Select the *one statement* that best describes the person's ability to read.

..... 3. Reads simple stories or comics.

..... 2. Reads various signs; e.g., No Parking, One Way, Women, Men, etc.

..... 1. Cannot read.

31. UNDERSTANDING OF COMPLEX INSTRUCTIONS: Select the *one statement* that best describes the person's ability to understand complex instructions.

..... 3. Understands instructions containing prepositions; e.g., on, in, behind, under, etc.

..... 2. Understands instructions requiring a simple decision: "If . . . , do this, but if not, do . . . ."

..... 1. Cannot comprehend any but simplest instructions.

32. POLITENESS AND SOCIABILITY: Select the *one statement* that best describes the person's ability to be polite and sociable.

..... 3. Uses phrases such as "please," and "thank you" and is sociable.

..... 2. Does not communicate to others about sports, family, group activities, etc. Communication is about self or wants.

..... 1. Insensitive to presence of other people.

33. GENERAL LANGUAGE DEVELOPMENT: Select the *one statement* that best describes the person's language development.

..... 3. Listens and can be reasoned with verbally and seems to enjoy social conversation.

..... 2. Converses, but reluctantly.

..... 1. Does not engage in conversation and avoids speaking to others.

34. NUMBER CONCEPT: Select the *one statement* that best describes the person's language development.

..... 3. Can use numbers up to ten (including addition and subtraction).

..... 2. Counts to thirty or more objects.

..... 1. Has little or no understanding of numbers.

Part III: SECONDARY FUNCTIONS

35. BED MAKING: Select the *one statement* that best describes the person's ability to make a bed.

..... 3. Makes bed correctly without supervision.

..... 2. Makes bed correctly with some help.

..... 1. Does not attempt to make the bed.

36. ROOM CLEANING: Select the *one statement* that best describes the person's house cleaning ability.

..... 3. Helps clean room well, including sweeping, dusting, and tidying up.

..... 2. Cleans room, but does not sweep under furniture, does not dust thoroughly, and requires supervision.

..... 1. Does not help clean rooms at all.

37. CARE OF CLOTHING: Select the *one statement* that best describes the person's care of clothing.

..... 3. Puts clothes in drawer or chest neatly and sends clothes to laundry without being reminded.

..... 2. Does not hang up clothes or put them away without being reminded.

..... 1. Does not hang up clothes even if reminded; has to be "picked up" after.

38. SENSE OF DIRECTION: Select the *one statement* that best describes the person's sense of direction.

..... 3. Can go around the Center grounds or several blocks from the Center without getting lost.

..... 2. Can go around the Center grounds or to a cottage or community facility with some help.

..... 1. Gets lost whenever he leaves his own living area.

39. HELPFULNESS AROUND COTTAGE: Select the *one statement* that best describes the person's ability to help around the cottage.

..... 3. Pitches in and shares cottage duties.

..... 2. Will work only when under direct supervision.

..... 1. Incapable of sharing or participating in keeping cottage livable.

40. TABLE SETTING: Select the *one statement* that best describes the person's ability to set the table.

..... 3. Could place all eating utensils, as well as napkins, salt pepper, sugar, etc., in positions he has learned.

..... 2. Could simply place silver, plates, cups, etc., on the table

..... 1. Cannot set table at all.

41. FOOD PREPARATION: Select the *one statement* that best describes the person's ability to cook. (not applicable to all)

..... 3. Could mix and cook simple food; e.g., frying eggs, making pancakes, etc.

..... 2. Could prepare simple foods requiring no mixing or cooking; e.g., making sandwiches, preparing cold cereal, etc.

..... 1. Cannot prepare food at all.

42. TABLE CLEARING: Select the *one statement* that best describes the person's ability to clear the table.

..... 3. Could clear table of breakable dishes and glassware.

..... 2. Could clear table of unbreakable dishes and silverware.

..... 1. Cannot clear table at all.

43. WORK FITNESS: Select the *one statement* that best describes the person's work fitness.

..... 3. Can perform a job requiring use of tools or machinery; e.g., shop work, sewing, etc.

..... 2. Can perform simple work; e.g., simple gardening, mopping floors, emptying trash, etc.

..... 1. Can perform no work at all.

44. JOB PERFORMANCE: Select the *one statement* that best describes the person's job performance.

..... 3. Job performance is satisfactory.

..... 2. Is a very slow worker and requires supervision.

..... 1. Does sloppy, inaccurate work or no work at all.

45. WORK HABITS: Select the *one statement* that best describes the person's work habits.

..... 3. Is on time for work, is seldom absent, needs very little supervision.

..... 2. Completes jobs with constant encouragement and supervision.

..... 1. Leaves work station without permission, or is not working.

46. INITIATIVE: Select the *one statement* that best describes the person's initiative.

..... 3. Initiates most of his own activities or asks for work.

..... 2. Sits all day if not directed to any activity.

..... 1. Will not do any assigned duties.

47. SELF-DIRECTION: Select the *one statement* that best describes the person's self-direction.

..... 3. Has ambition and interest in things.

..... 2. Seems to have no interest in things.

..... 1. Is unnecessarily dependent on others for help.

48. PERSISTENCE: Select the *one statement* that best describes the person's persistence.

..... 3. Does not discourage easily.

..... 2. Needs constant encouragement to work at a task.

..... 1. Jumps from one activity to another and never finishes a task.

49. PERSEVERANCE: Select the *one statement* that best describes the person's perseverance.

..... 3. Will pay attention to a task for *more than* 15 minutes; e.g., cleaning up, putting things away.

..... 2. Will pay attention to a task for at least 5 minutes.

..... 1. Will not pay attention to a task, even if it requires *less than* 5 minutes.

50. ORGANIZATION OF OWN LEISURE TIME ACTIVITY: Select the *one statement* that best describes the person's own leisure time activity.

..... 3. Organizes leisure time on a fairly complex level; e.g., selects activities.

..... 2. Organizes leisure time adequately on a simple level; e.g., watching television, listening to phonograph or radio, participation in planned events.

..... 1. Will not join in leisure time activity unless encouraged.

51. GENERAL SELF-DIRECTION: Select the *one statement* that best describes the person's ability of self-direction. (minimal supervision)

..... 3. Concentrates on tasks and usually carries them through to completion.

..... 2. Does simple work only. Needs reassignment at the completion of each task.

..... 1. Cannot maintain self on any work.

52. RESPONSIBILITY FOR PERSONAL BELONGINGS: Select the *one statement* that best describes the person's *highest* level of responsibility for personal belongings; e.g., clothing, books, pencils, etc.

..... 3. Very dependable—always takes care of personal belongings.

..... 2. Usually dependable—reasonably certain that the person takes care of personal belongings.

..... 1. Not responsible at all—does not take care of personal belongings.

53. RESPONSIBILITY: Select the *one statement* that best describes the person's *highest* level of responsibility.

..... 3. Very conscientious and assumes much responsibility—makes a special effort; the assigned act will always be performed.

..... 2. Usually dependable—makes an effort to carry out responsibility; one can be reasonably certain that the assigned act will be performed.

..... 1. Not given responsibility; is unable to carry out responsibility at all.

54. COOPERATIVENESS: Select the *one statement* that best describes the person's ability to be cooperative.

..... 3. Offers assistance to others.

..... 2. Does helpful things for others if asked to do so.

.....1. Does not care to help others.

55. CONSIDERATION OF OTHERS: Select the *one statement* that best describes the person's consideration of others.

..... 3. Offers assistance to others; is not indifferent.

..... 2. Does helpful things for others if asked to do so.

..... 1. Disinterested in others.

56. KNOWLEDGE ABOUT OTHERS: Select the *one statement* that best describes the person's knowledge of others.

..... 3. Recognizes own family and faces of others; e.g., ward personnel, classmates, staff, etc.

..... 2. Does not know many persons in the Center; e.g., ward personnel, cottage mates.

..... 1. Keeps to self and does not relate to others.

57. INTERACTION WITH OTHERS: Select the *one statement* that best describes the person's *highest* level of interaction with others.

..... 3. Plays cooperatively or competitively with others in group games.

..... 2. Plays with others for at least short periods of time; e.g., showing or offering toys, clothing, or object.

..... 1. Is completely unresponsive to others.

58. PARTICIPATION IN GROUP ACTIVITIES: Select the *one statement* that best describes the person's *highest* level of participation in group activities.

..... 3. Initiates group activities (leader and organizer).

..... 2. Participates in group activities spontaneously and eagerly (active participant).

..... 1. Does not participate in group activities (an isolate).

59. SELFISHNESS: Select the *one statement* that best describes the person's selfishness.

..... 3. Does share with others.

..... 2. Shares, but reluctantly.

..... 1. Expects everyone to give in to his wishes.

60. SOCIALIZATION: Select the *one statement* that best describes the person's ability to socialize.

..... 3. Does anything to make friends.

..... 2. Does not make friends easily but is approachable.

..... 1. Rejects friendship.

J. McV. Hunt

Psychological Assessment, Developmental Plasticity, and Heredity, With Implications for Early Education

EVIDENCE FROM COMPARATIVE LINGUISTICS convinced Benjamin Whorf (1956) that language does a great deal to shape thought and understanding. Although the topic of this book is cognitive development, our concern is with what we currently term mental retardation. This term seems to indicate that something in the mind has slowed or lagged. It makes time per se the central factor in the development of mind. This was never the case. When I was taking graduate courses instead of teaching them, the prevailing term for the set of conditions now subsumed under mental retardation was feebleminded, or if one wished a fancy term with Greek roots, *oligophrenia,* which also means weak-minded.

Euphemisms are the rule in the semantics of behavioral defects. Although both "weakness" and "retardation" imply defect, this shift in terminology, for which we psychologists are responsible in large measure, carries a substantial shift in our conception of what influences behavior. I suppose the empirical grounds for this shift were laid by Binet and Simon when they first noted a rough correlation of competence on their tests of judgment, comprehension,

J. McV. Hunt, Ph.D., is professor of psychology at the University of Illinois.

and reasoning with age. From this rough correlation came their term mental age. This shift in emphasis from weakness of mind to delay in development received further support in 1912 when Wilhelm Stern suggested dividing mental age (MA) by chronological age to get the intelligence quotient (IQ). Stern made this suggestion on the assumption that the rate of development is a fundamental trait in which individuals differ. This shift in emphasis got fixed in our culture when, in the 1920s and 1930s, IQs and mental ages based on Terman's 1916 revision and standardization of the Binet scales began to provide the legal limits for what theretofore had been the loosely defined terms of moron (IQ: 50 to 75, or MA: 8 to 12 years), imbecile (IQ: 12 to 49, or MA: 2 to 7 years), and idiot (IQ less than 20, or MA less than 2 years). When Arnold Gesell's descriptions of the behavior typical of successive ages became widely disseminated, these descriptions habituated the notion that development comes more or less automatically with age. Despite the controversy over the developmental constancy of the IQ, this habit of thought about the role of time in development and about the longitudinal predictive value of IQs has become strong and persistent.

During the past decade we have been encountering some unhappy consequences of this habit of thought. Outside professional circles of psychology and education, people in various minority groups have rebelled against the implication that an hour's performance in an artificial testing situation could demonstrate and prove the inevitable and permanent retarded inferiority of their children. They have made their rebellion felt. Within the profession, moreover, habits of thought about the IQ have led to disappointment and confusion when gains in IQ from special educational programs shortly disappeared after the gainers were returned to their original home and school environments.

Such obviously unhappy consequences are, I believe, but the visible portion of an iceberg of misconception. Less obvious but perhaps more unfortunate are other consequences. Exceedingly unfortunate are the fates of those children whose low scores on IQ tests have led their teachers to expect little learning from them and therefore to use little teaching ingenuity in their behalf. Just as unfortunate is the failure of tests of intelligence to provide helpful information for selecting curricular materials to promote development and learning. Most unfortunate of all, perhaps, is the false confidence in a view of intelligence as a kind of power in which individuals differ consistently regardless of the circumstances of their lives. The process of measuring this power by comparing the test scores of individuals, moreover, has probably greatly increased the tendency toward competitiveness in our society. Comparative rankings and competitiveness are probably inevitable in human affairs. A degree of competitiveness is highly desirable, but assessing development by way of individual differences has exaggerated this proneness to competitiveness and distracted both parents and teachers from focusing on what is to be learned and on the task of encouraging the development of the young. This comparative approach to assessment has tended to prevent educators and psychologists from concerning themselves with the concrete nature of the intelligence and motivation underlying competence as a hierarchy of learning sets, of strategies for processing information, of concepts, and of skills built up sequentially in ordinal fashion. The false confidence in a view of intelligence as a kind of facultylike power has stood in the way of investigating the implications of this hierarchical view. Thus, if the obviously unhappy consequences of what has become our traditional habit of thought in this domain call forth a conceptual revision, that will be splendid. This revision should lead, I believe, to a new strategy in the assessment or measurement of psychological development and of competence which, hopefully, will encourage rather than discourage ingenuity in teaching.

Toward a Revised Conception of Intelligence

Over a decade ago, in *Intelligence and Experience* (Hunt, 1961), I tried to alter our habits of thought about cognitive development and intelligence with both argument and evidence. On the side of argument I contended that IQ scores on tests of intelligence are valid only as an assessment of past acquisitions, that they have very little validity as predictors of future IQs or performances without knowledge of the circumstances to be encountered. I suggested that we should think of psychological development and of intelligence as a hierarchy of learning sets, strategies of information processing, concepts, motivational systems, and skills acquired in the course of each child's ongoing interaction, and especially informational interaction, with his environmental circumstances. On the side of evidence I reviewed a substantial body of investigative results indicating a great deal of plasticity in psychological development. From these several lines of evidence and argument, I suggested that readiness is no mere matter of maturation that occurs automatically with living to a given age. Rather, it is a matter of information stored, of concepts, strategies, and motivational systems achieved, and of skills acquired. I also introduced what I like to call *"the problem of the match,"* which I later elaborated (Hunt, 1963a, 1965, 1966). This is a problem especially for parents and teachers and for all those who wish to foster psychological development in the young. The nature of the problem is based on the idea that adaptive growth takes place only, or at least chiefly, in situations that contain for any given infant or child information and models just discrepant enough from those already stored and mastered to produce interest or challenge and to call for adaptive modifications in the structure of his intellectual coping, in his beliefs about the world, and in the motor patterns that are not beyond his adaptive capacity at the time.

Theorizing and investigating relevant to these views during the past decade have strengthened them and suggested elaborations. Let me mention a few of these theoretical developments and bits of evidence.

The decade brought L. G. Humphrey's (1962a) demonstration-argument that tests of intelligence are basically like tests of achievement in that both call upon previously acquired percepts, concepts, motives, and skills. The fact that the tests of intelligence call for older acquisitions for which the learning situations are more difficult to specify than do achievement tests does not destroy the basic similarity. Humphreys (1962b) extended G. A. Ferguson's (1956, 1959) explanation of the ability factors derived from factor analysis in terms of positive transfer of training by showing how the experimental manipulations that have traditionally been used to study the transfer of training can account for the obtained nodes of intercorrelation among abilities. Although these analyses provide a clear theoretical basis for an important role of experience in the development of intelligence as it has been traditionally measured and analyzed, they provide little guidance for parents and teachers in understanding how interests and abilities build dynamically upon one another and in choosing the circumstances best calculated to foster the development of new levels of ability in children.

My notion of the "problem of the match" and its later elaborations (Hunt, 1963a, 1965, 1966) make cognitive acquisitions of central importance for development in other domains, especially for motivation. This notion has received considerable support. Several studies by my own group of attentional preference in very young infants have lent support to the theory that emerging recognitive familiarity motivates the maintenance of perceptual contact with whatever is becoming perceptually recognizable (Hunt, 1970; Uzgiris & Hunt, 1970; Greenberg, Uzgiris, & Hunt, 1970; Weizmann, Cohen, & Pratt, 1971). The motivational import of what is becoming recognitively familiar is less a stage of psychological development, however, than a phase in the course of information processing. This is suggested by a still tentative finding that when infants nearly a year old are regularly presented with pairs of patterns in tests of four minutes, and one pattern is presented regularly test after test and another intermittently every seventh test, the infants look longer at the regularly presented patterns before (i.e., after fewer tests) they look longer at the intermittently presented patterns (Paraskevopoulos & Hunt, 1971). Other observational evidence came in the course of developing our ordinal scale of imitation (Uzgiris & Hunt, 1966, 1968). Our observation that infants regularly showed pseudoimitation of highly familiar gestural and vocal patterns before they imitated unfamiliar ones suggests this same course of development. Our observations, moreover, indicated great motivational importance for the match between the model presented and the previous achievements of the infant. Infants are strongly motivated to imitate only models that challenge to a proper degree their perceptual and cognitive grasp or their motor skills. They withdraw from models too "old hat" or simple out of apparent boredom. They become distressed and angry with models that call for either cognitive or motor adaptations beyond their abilities. I believe we can say that an infant will imitate only what he can understand, so what he does toward imitating a given model often shows what he understands of that model or how he sees it.

Other bits of evidence supporting this view that cognitive developments are important to development in various other domains such as emotion and motivation have come from investigations in other laboratories. The role of cognitive achievement in behavior indicative of emotion is illustrated in a very recent study by T. R. Schultz and E. Zigler (1971). On the assumption that a clown presented in a stationary condition would be easier to assimilate perceptually than the same clown in motion, because of the difficulty in following contours, Schultz and Zigler predicted that such expressions of pleasure as visual fixation, smiling, and nonstressful vocalizing would occur earlier for the stationary than for the moving condition. The findings clearly confirmed this prediction. The role of cognitive achievement in motivation is illustrated in the finding by Zigler, J. Levine, and L. Gould (1967) that children of school age appreciate and prefer cartoons near the upper limit of their comprehension. In my own theorizing (Hunt, 1965) I have suggested that the self-concept, and especially the ideal self-concept, may well be the most important cognitive construct for the motivation of achievement and social behavior. It was especially interesting, therefore, to find P. Katz and Zigler (1967) suggesting that the disparity between the concepts of self and ideal self should be related to developmental maturity because such maturity involves capacity for cognitive differentiation. Their finding of positive associations of both chronological age and IQ with the size of the disparities between the self and the ideal self supports this contention that cognitive development is important in other domains, especially in motivation. In this same vein, L. Kohlberg and Zigler (1967) have suggested that a child's concept of his sex role results largely from having categorized himself as either male or female early in development. Inasmuch as cognitive development involves transformations of the mental constructions of a child's environment, they reason that both mental age and IQ should be positively correlated with maturity of social development, and they found mature trends in social development coming earlier in children with above average IQs than in children with average IQs.

The Issue of Motivational Autonomy

These findings support the contention that developments within the cognitive domain are important for development in other domains of psychological development; however, they also raise some questions. Seldom do the gains on tests of intelligence and achievement from various systems of compensatory education persist once the children are returned to the environments of their homes and standard schools. From the traditional view of essentially predetermined maturation and development, one could argue that these gains have been obtained only in the limited cognitive skills assessed and that development in the other domains awaits maturation of the organism as a whole. Inasmuch as the evidence that I shall shortly synopsize suggests that maturation itself shows considerable plasticity, I question seriously such an explanation. I suspect that the failure of the gains from so many systems of compensatory education to persist resides rather in the failure of these systems to provide experiences calculated to inculcate ideal self-concepts. These self-concepts include professed ability to learn readily and pride in such learning, which yield autonomous striving.

It is likely that such motivational systems have their developmental beginnings very early. Burton White (1971) has found that the behavioral patterns of outstanding overall competence are already present in children by age three. He is now emphasizing the importance of the period between the ages of ten months and three years in early home-based education. Inasmuch as evidences of great plasticity exist in various lines of development during the first year, however, this finding is probably based on cultural practices of child rearing during the first year, which differ relatively little from home to home and class to class. During the period from ten months to three years in age, however, when the burgeoning capacities of infants for manipulation and locomotion put considerable stress on mothers, the child rearing across homes probably differs enough to show prominently in the competence of the young by age three. Observations of the joy that infants of only two months show in connection with making a mobile sway by shaking themselves (Hunt & Uzgiris, 1964; Uzgiris & Hunt, 1970) and similar observations (Watson, 1966, 1967) suggest that the beginnings of the motivation to act upon the world to achieve ends anticipated by the infant begins very early indeed. Robert White (1959) has characterized such motivation by the term competence and contended that it is an associated emotion, which he calls effectance. I have attempted to describe a mechanism for such motivation inherent in information processing and action (Hunt, 1960; 1963b; 1965; 1971a, Ch. 4; 1971b, Ch. 5).

The importance of perceptual feedback to action in such early development has been illustrated in a study reported last March by L. J. Yarrow, J. L. Rubenstein, and F. A. Pedersen (1971) at the Society for Research in Child Development. This system of motivation (called goal orientation in this study) was assessed in infants at six months of age by a cluster of six items on the Bayley scales, which included some persistent and purposeful attempts to secure objects out of reach. Highly consonant with the view I have described is that the measure of goal orientation correlated +0.38 with maternal responsiveness to their infants' expressions of distress. According to standard operant theory with its emphasis on overt behavior, the contingency of maternal response to such distress behaviors as crying should reinforce those overt behaviors. It did not. In such young infants, apparently, the contingency of maternal response to distressful vocalization reinforces hope of change in the circumstances and contributes toward a general level of confidence on the part of the infant that he can control his circumstances. Such is the epigenesis of early development that later, however, such a contingency would reinforce the overt crying. Out of such experiences of being able to change conditions comes gradually, I suspect, a kind of learning set that we (not the infant) might verbalize as: "If I act, I can get what I want and make interesting things happen." I contend that this learning set is basically cognitive in character. It is knowledge of infant self in relation to the world. If the child has tried and tried to no avail, he derives another kind of learning set that must be corrected if he is ever to achieve confidence and hope that he can achieve his ends and to develop the pride of achievement that leads to the achievement of excellence in performance.

We know all too little about the successive landmarks in the development of these learning sets and concepts with motivational significance. Because we have thought of cognition largely in terms of such school skills as language or reading or numbering, our various systems of compensatory education have omitted even any attempt to provide corrective experiences of significance for motivation. Years ago Andras Angyal (1941) described and emphasized a general dynamic trend toward increasing autonomy in psychological development. We need to know more about fostering such motivational autonomy and more about how long it takes.

Maturation and Experience

In our various conceptions of development, learning and

maturation have been as separate conceptually and presumably in actuality as Rudyard Kipling's East and West. The decade just past, however, has brought clear evidence that informational interaction, especially encounters perceived visually, influences maturation within the central nervous system. Studies of the effects of early perceptual experience on maze learning in rats and dogs, inspired by D. O. Hebb's (1949) theorizing, go back to the decade of the 1950s (see Hunt, 1961, pp. 100-106). A. H. Riesen, also inspired by Hebb's theorizing, first reported even earlier (Riesen, 1947, 1958) the effects of rearing chimpanzees in the dark on the number of nerve cells and glial cells in their retinal ganglia as adults. And S. O. Brattgård (1952), inspired by the biochemical theorizing of Helgar Hydén, reported that rearing rabbits in the dark caused a paucity of RNA production of their retinal ganglia as adults. Since then, the California group (Bennett, Diamond, Krech, & Rosenzweig, 1964; Krech, Rosenzweig, & Bennett, 1966) has reported that thickness of the cerebral cortex and the level of total acetylcholine esterase activity of the cortex as well as rate of adult maze learning are a function of the complexity of the environment during early life. Studies of the effects of rearing in the dark during early life have been extended back into the visual system. Such rearing in the dark produces a paucity of both cells and glial fibers in the lateral geniculate body of the thalamus (Wiesel & Hubel, 1963). And, as the Spanish investigator F. Valverde has shown, rearing in the dark also decreases both dendritic branching and the number of spines that develop on the dendritic processes of the large apical cells of the striate area in the occipital lobes in mice (Valverde, 1967, 1968; Valverde & Esteban, 1968). Valverde's approach should now be extended to the coordination of the visual system with other systems. Such evidence strongly suggests considerable plasticity in the maturation of the neuroanatomical equipment for information processing.

Spurious Factors in Longitudinal Validity

Intelligence testing has assumed approximately equal opportunity for learning, at least in typical families. Studies during the past decade have showed vast variations in the opportunities for the basic nutritional requirements for development, in the opportunities to acquire cognitive skills, in the opportunities to develop the motivational systems required for competence, and in the opportunities to acquire those values and standards of conduct required by a complex, organized society (Hunt, 1969, pp. 202-214). Such opportunities are lacking most often for children of the poor, but Burton White (1971) has found that some of the mothers within the poverty sector are the most effective infant teachers in Aid to Dependent Children. Moreover, we all know children in middle-class families whose opportunities are limited in various ways by ineffective mothering.

Results from other recent studies have raised methodological issues that depress the traditional importance of longitudinal validity coefficients for the IQ. The evidence of plasticity in early development has been compelling, at least to me, yet both psychologists and educators ask almost regularly about the predictive value of the measures of development from the ordinal scales that Uzgiris and I have developed. It seems likely that the failure of the evidence for plasticity to be more widely convincing resides in the longitudinal validity correlations between the IQs from testings widely separated in time. B. S. Bloom (1964) based much of his discussion of stability and change on such evidence. It has been presumed generally that the basis for the existence of such correlations resides within the individual differences in the rates of development for the tested individuals. This is, to be sure, one source of the obtained coefficients, but there are, I believe, at least two other sources that are spurious for such an interpretation.

If tests of intelligence measure achievement, as I believe Humphreys (1962a) has demonstrated, then the correlation between successive testings involves part to whole relations in which the size of the part in the first testing approaches the size of the whole in the latter testing as the time between the testings decreases (Humphreys, 1962b). The portion of a longitudinal validity coefficient deriving from this part to whole relation is completely irrelevant to any assumption of inherent stability in rates of individual development.

The second spurious factor in these longitudinal correlations is found in the consistency of developmental impact of home and neighborhood environments. [The recent investigation by Yarrow et al. (1971) is relevant here.] Pedersen reports that measures of home environments—social and inanimate—which were based on two three-hour time samplings taken a week apart show correlations with various measures of performance from the Bayley scales ranging to above 0.5, thereby accounting for 25 percent of the variance in the measures of infant performance at age six months. If merely two three-hour samples a week apart can represent the impact of environmental circumstances for the first half year of the lives of infants sufficiently well to account for 25 percent of the variance in any of their performances at six months, then the consistency in the developmental impact of home environments is much greater than we have ever conceived such consistency to be. Whatever portion of the longitudinal validity coefficient derives from this consistency in the developmental impact of home environments is entirely spurious as an indicator of inherent individual differences in rate of maturation. These spurious contributions from the part to whole relations and from the consistency in the developmental impact in the environment subtract substantially from the traditional import of the longitudinal validity coefficients for the IQ.

Revised Strategies of Measurement

In his lectures *On Understanding Science,* J. B. Conant (1947, p. 48) "put down as one of the principles learned from the history of science that a theory is only overthrown by a better theory, never merely by contradictory facts." I believe Conant might have added that, whenever strategy and technology of measurement are imbedded in a prevailing conceptual scheme, it becomes additionally difficult to revise that conceptual scheme with a combination of both evidence dissonant with it and new conceptual alternatives. The tests of intelligence are generally recognized as one of the great monuments of achievement by modern psychology. Yet, as I have already pointed out, they have left many problems in psychological development unsolved and have even distracted attention from them. For three-quarters of a century they have focused attention on comparative measures of individual differences in a power (the IQ or Spearman's *g*) or a multiplicity of powers (Thurstone, 1938; Guilford, 1967). I believe this focus has distracted investigators from seeing how in the various lines of psychological development the actual landmarks of ability and of motivation build upon one another. I believe this focus has also distracted investigators from investigating the nature of the successive learning sets that enable and motivate a child to process information and to solve problems at successive levels of complexity. Instead of helping to tell teachers how to prepare the curricular environment to foster the development of any given child, the scores from the tests have tended to destroy the motivation for ingenuity in teaching by explaining poor pupil performance as "to be expected." Fortunately, the beginnings of new strategies for the measurement of learning and development are appearing.

One of these new strategies consists of criterion-referenced tests (Glaser, 1963). This strategy is derived from the hierarchical conception of intelligence suggested by R. M. Gagné's studies of adult problem solving (Gagné & Paradise, 1961). In this strategy R. Glaser (Glaser, 1963; Glaser & Nitko, 1971) contrasts the criterion reference with the norm reference, which is characteristic of the standard test batteries for both intelligence and achievement. For traditional norm-referenced tests, the performance of an individual acquires its meaning from some index of its comparative rank among the scores describing the performances of the various individuals in the representative group on which the norms for the test are based. For criterion-referenced tests, on the other hand, the meaning of any individual's performance derives directly from the behavioral goal of the educational experience that has been provided for him. This behavioral goal defines the performance desired of the tested subject, and his performance, in turn, determines the criterion of success for the educational effort. This strategy of criterion referencing gives new meaning to the standard concepts of reliability and validity for test scores (Popham & Husek, 1969). Reliability derives from examiner agreement, and validity is inherent in the relation between the examinee's performance and the educational goal. Thus, this strategy also has the very considerable advantage of focusing the attention and effort of both teacher and student upon the goal of the educational effort and of avoiding the distraction that is almost inevitable from the interpersonal comparisons involved in norm referencing. Missing from such a strategy, however, is any developmental frame of reference that can help explain failure and help guide a teacher in choosing learning experiences. We might also note that age and time do not figure at all in this strategy of measurement.

The second new strategy consists of ordinal scales of psychological development. This strategy is at least illustrated by our own ordinal scales of development in infancy (Uzgiris & Hunt, 1966, 1968). These scales, inspired by Jean Piaget's (1936, 1937) observations of his own three children, consist of sequentially ordinal landmarks for six overlapping lines of development through what Piaget has termed the sensorimotor phase. Each landmark is specified behavior elicited by a specified situation. Interobserver agreement on the criterion behaviors is typically above 95 percent. Test-retest consistency for examinations conducted within 48 hours is typically above 85 percent, and the great majority of the changes that occur are upward on the scales. The ordinality of the steps on the various scales as indicated by B. F. Green's (1956) index of consistency range from a low of 0.802, for the scale on the development of relation to objects, to a high of 0.991, for the scale on the construction of operational causality. For all but two of our six scales, Green's index of consistency is well above 0.9. In some instances, the invariance in sequence is logically built in; but, contrary to the argument of Mary Shirley (1931), such invariance of sequence need logically imply no predetermined maturation. It is basically a function of the infant's informational interactions with his environment. These interactions produce developments that permit other higher-order forms of informational interaction.

The sequential ordinality of steps in these scales provides a novel strategy for the measurement of psychological development. We can compare the development of two infants, regardless of their ages, in terms of their positions on each of the scales. This ordinality permits us to reverse the traditional strategy of measuring psychological development by making age the dependent variable that varies as a function of kind of experience instead of the independent variable implied in our traditional concept of the IQ and of the normative descriptions of Arnold Gesell et al. (1940). These sequentially ordinal landmarks permit us to define successive levels of development in terms of success on lower landmarks on the scale and failure on those above. We then can compare the means and variances of age for infants who have lived from birth under differing kinds of circumstances. These variations in age permit us to compare the educational, or development fostering, quality of these differing circumstances. Such measures based on ordinal scales may have the additional value of referring only to past experience and of making no claims of persistence in the rate of development.

Ordinal landmarks in development need imply no position on the issue concerning whether psychological development occurs continuously or in steps. We have identified more landmarks than the six sensorimotor stages described by Piaget. Our scale of object permanence, for instance, consists of fourteen sequentially ordinal landmarks. From the evidence with which I an now acquainted, I believe that psychological development is continuous and that high consistency values for measures of sequential ordinality are a function of selecting behavioral landmarks with sufficient distance between them. This domain is wide open for investigation. The landmarks that we have selected are little more than first approximations of what can ultimately be derived from exploring behavioral development with such a strategy. If we are ever to have the basis for guiding the learning of the young in what Piaget has termed the preconceptual phase, I believe this strategy must be extended through this phase. I suspect that investigations might be especially fruitful in providing the evidences of effectiveness for new educational efforts with pathologically retarded children.

It should be noted that the examining operations that define the sequentially achieved landmarks in development resemble criterion-referenced tests. In neither case does the meaning of an individual child's performance derive from comparison with the performance of others. In ordinal scales of psychological development, however, there is no educational experience with a behavioral goal to give meaning to the performance. Once the sequentially achieved landmarks have been identified, the meaning of any child's performance derives from where that performance places him along the sequentially ordinal scale.

New Evidence of Plasticity

The ordinal strategy of assessing psychological development is beginning to yield new evidence of plasticity. In a recent article (Hunt, 1971c) I discussed the finding that providing very young infants with stabile patterns over their cribs to look at for at least a half an hour each day has reduced the age at which the blink response appears by somewhat more than three weeks (Greenberg, Uzgiris, & Hunt, 1968). In this same article I also called attention to Burton White's (1967) experimental demonstration that experiential enrichments in which the chief factor appears to have been the opportunity to view stabiles of complexity adjusted to the infant's level of development very substantially reduced median ages for "fisted swiping" and "mature reaching," two of the outstanding landmarks in the development of eye and hand coordination. For mature reaching, the change in median age was from 145 days to 89 days.

This result implies that what geneticists, since the days of Waltereck (Dunn, 1965), have termed the norm of reaction for the age at which this landmark appears must be at least the 56 days by which these two medians differ.

Neither the blink response nor eye and hand coordination are very general or instrumental to later development. Neither are they within the domain of what we usually think of as cognitive. On the other hand, I believe that object construction is all three, and I believe that imitation is within the domain of cognition and that it is motivationally instrumental to later development. Using the scales of object permanence and both gestural and vocal imitation, we have recently examined all the children between five months and five years of age who have lived from birth in two Athenian orphanages with differing regimes of child rearing (Paraskevopoulos & Hunt, 1971). The difference between the regimes of child rearing can most easily be specified in terms of the child to caretaker ratio. In the Municipal Orphanage this ratio is of the order of 10/1. In the other orphanage, the Metera Baby Centre, which attempts to be a model institution for children, this ratio is on the average through the day approximately 3/1 or 4/1. We also examined some 94 home-reared children from working-class families. The mean ages for the children at the Municipal Orphanage lagged progressively for those at successive levels of object permanence. Let me take, for example, that level at which children follow an object through one hidden displacement but not through a series of such displacements. The mean ages of the children at this level in the Municipal Orphanage was 33.2 months, of those at Metera, 21.8 months, and of those home reared, 20.3 months. The mean for the children at the Municipal Orphanage differs significantly from both those at Metera and those reared at home. As an empirical estimate of the age norm of reaction for this level of object permanence, the mean ages for infants in these two orphanages are but a part of the picture. David Schickedanz has been following the development of infants in the Parent-and-Child Center at Mount Carmel, Illinois. Six successive infants from parents of poverty who have been developing under the regime there, which I shall characterize shortly, have achieved this level of following an object through one hidden displacement before they were a year old. Their average age would be approximately 11.5 months. Thus, the norm of reaction of this level of object construction must be at least of the order of 21 months. Similar norms of reaction exist for the ages at which children achieve the upper levels of vocal imitation. Clearly the circumstances encountered by children can make a very substantial difference in the ages at which such early intellectual and motivational landmarks are achieved. How important various degrees of lag are in such early development for future development remains for investigation. Perhaps I should note here also that, unless my clinical hunch is far afield, language development demands having achieved both object construction through hidden displacements and the development of an interest in imitating unfamiliar vocal patterns. In order to disabuse myself as soon as possible of a mistaken hypothesis, I am now looking for children who have begun to speak who lack one or the other of these achievements. How object construction and language are related in blind children deserves special scrutiny in this connection. I should also note in passing that it is hard not to view differences in ability to communicate as a result of the differences in social interaction and child-rearing practices in various social classes (Hunt, 1969, Ch. 7).

A methodological implication should be mentioned here. Neither the traditional cross-sectional strategy of assessing development in differing groups nor traditional longitudinal investigation that follows the development of individuals within a given ecological niche can yield the kinds of information we need about the relation of psychological development to environmental encounters for purposes of child rearing and education. What we need is to combine the longitudinal approach with the experimental, or quasi-experimental, by following longitudinally the development of comparable groups of genotypes developing under differing conditions. In this connection, simultaneously contemporary experimental and control groups are probably unfeasible, but we can use wave design with successive groups developing under progressively enriched conditions.

Plasticity and Heredity

In this discussion I have been using the genetic concept of the norm of reaction. This concept should be more familiar to educators and psychologists who are typically so concerned with the pseudoissue of whether environment or heredity is more important that they make two common conceptual errors. First, as J. Hirsch (1970), the behavioral geneticist, has pointed out, these persons typically test groups of individuals at a single time of life. The resulting proportions of the variance assigned to environment and to heredity concern the relative amounts of variance among individuals developing within a given range of variation in circumstances. Such assessments of variance are then applied quite incorrectly to individuals. Secondly, these assessments of variance among individuals or comparable statistical indices of heritability are used to make inferences about the educability of individuals. The educability of an individual calls for solid evidence about the norm of reaction. But a statistical index of heritability, to quote Hirsch (1970, p. 101), "provides no information about the norm of reaction."

Concern with this pseudoissue of whether environment or heredity is more important gets those who find and point out the evidences of plasticity in phenotypic measures of intellectual and motivational development tarred with the opprobrious semantic brush of environmentalism. I wish to point out that evidences of plasticity are not dissonant with a primary role for heredity. Heredity is always primary. The genotype in the fertilized ovum constitutes the starting point for an individual. The DNA in the genes contains information that sets the main lines of development throughout life, yet this information goes nowhere in an environmental vacuum and gets modified by variations in different environmental conditions. This DNA is far from totally predetermining. Development comes dynamically in the course of a continuing process of interaction between the individual at any given time and his environmental circumstances at that given time. The resulting norm or range of reaction is great for most of the traits in which educators and psychologists are interested. Even so, heredity remains primary in determining the size of the differences between the phenotypic measures that will come from any two sets of differing circumstances. One might put this principle more simply by saying that the genotype determines the norm of reaction. Unfortunately, such a statement is scientifically meaningless because neither the genotype nor the ultimate norm of reaction is measurable and knowable.

For concretely illustrating this principle, suppose, for example, the existence of two pairs of identical twins, one pair typical or normal, the other mongoloid. Suppose one of each pair was reared from birth in the Municipal Orphanage of Athens where neither becomes a pet of the caretaker. Suppose the other is reared in Metera under the carefully supervised regime there. Which pair would show the greater difference in age of achieving that level of object construction in which it follows an object through one hidden displacement but not several? I believe you will agree that the difference in age to be expected for the normal pair will be greater than that for the mongoloid pair. I have designated one pair as mongoloid to permit recognition of the limitation on genotypic potential at birth. In principle, the same prediction should hold for pairs that differ in potential within the normal range. Thus, hypothetically at least, the genotype determines the amount of the effect on a phenotypic measure that ongoing interaction in two differing environments can have. The threshold conception of environmental influence, epitomized as "normal environmental conditions" in which this hypothetical threshold is regularly achieved in typical families, is likely to be very far from true. Evidence from the study by Paraskevopoulos and Hunt (1971), already cited, calls this position into serious question. This evidence derives from the standard deviations of the ages for the children at the higher levels of object construction and vocal imitation. As might be expected, the standard deviations for children who follow an object through one or more hidden displacements are smallest (approximately 2.5 months) for those children at Metera where the conditions of rearing are relatively standardized. At the Municipal Orphanage, where the child to caretaker ratio of 10/1 inevitably results in combinations of pets and neglected children, the standard deviation of ages for children at this same pair of levels are of the order of seven months; for the ages of home-reared children at these levels the standard deviations are even larger, though not significantly larger, than those for the Municipal Orphanage. These large standard deviations do not come from distributions composed of a cluster of cases at the lower end of the distribution with a single case or two at the high end as would be expected if the environment operates in threshold fashion.

Implications for the Mentally Retarded

The implications for the mentally retarded from the conceptual revisions and evidence I have outlined fall into two categories. One category consists of suggestions for fostering intellectual and motivational development for the retarded; and the other category is methodological, namely, that we utilize the interest which exists in those mentally retarded to get a better understanding of the nature of psychological development.

The fact that the babies of parents from the poverty sector at the Parent-and-Child Center in Mount Carmel, Illinois, are developing rapidly and happily, as evidenced by the early ages at which they are achieving the successive landmarks on our ordinal scales, suggests that what the caretaker-mothers of these children are being taught about child rearing is on at least a promising track. What they are being taught by Mrs. Earladeen Badger (1971, 1972) is conceptually quite simple. First, the mothers, who are also the caretakers in this Parent-and-Child Center, are encouraged strongly to believe that how they interact with and treat their babies will make an important difference in the future of the children. Second, they are encouraged, while their babies are very young, to be responsive to their behavioral indicators of distress. Third, they are taught to observe their infants in their interaction with models and play materials for behavioral indications of interest and surprise, of boredom, and of the distressful frustration that comes with situations with which the infant cannot cope. Fourth, they are encouraged to provide their infants with materials and models that arouse behavioral signs of interest and to remove those materials that appear to be either boring or threatening. Finally, they are shown enough about the sequences of developing abilities and interests to help them choose materials that will interest their infants.

In the course of teaching mothers and observing children, Mrs. Badger is gleaning a number of clinical suggestions about these developmental sequences extending beyond the sensorimotor into the preconceptual phase. For instance, once infants in their play with a shape box have achieved the level where they put the blocks of varying shapes in holes with appropriate shapes without active experimentation but merely from visual inspection, they can be happily interested in picture-matching games. On the other hand, while they are still struggling with a rectangular block in a square hole and a square block in the circular hole, any attempt to introduce picture-matching games is a source of threat and distress. Such procedures should be helpful in devising and testing educational strategies for fostering the psychological development of children with mental retardation based upon pathological heredity.

In the methodological category, if we once take seriously the concept of psychological development as a hierarchy of learning sets, strategies of information processing, and skills built one upon another in ordinal fashion, we must recognize that our ignorance of the details of its nature is abysmal. Two aspects of mental retardation suggest that mentally retarded children may be enabled to advance while simultaneously helping us to reduce our ignorance. Genotypically based difficulties in learning may actually be helpful in uncovering the nature of the hierarchy of learning sets and the special kinds of experience that foster their acquisition. In 1930 I spent nearly half an hour a day throughout the summer attempting unsuccessfully to teach an eight-year-old imbecile to count. Following suggestions derived from the writings of Fernald, my method was to attempt through repetition to get this boy to coordinate in time saying the successive numbers and pointing to one object after another. It failed. I suspect that I failed because I had not considered providing him with experiences that then would have seemed quite irrelevant to the learning task. At that time, it did not occur to me to consider or to look for understanding and skills propaedeutic to such a coordination as that between saying numbers and pointing to objects. Neither did I think of ways to make that coordination meaningful and important. Today, in both cases, these are things I would consider although I confess that the search might be difficult.

Secondly, the newfound and growing interest in mental retardation promises to provide the support for investigators interested in utilizing the educational process to investigate the nature of the hierarchical structure of competence in mentally retarded infants and young children. A decade of taking seriously the hierarchical conception of learning sets in psychological development and investigating its concrete nature will almost certainly yield knowledge that will greatly improve our technology of early education. After such a decade time per se will no longer loom so large as a cause of development. Perhaps we shall then have new terminology for what we now call mental retardation.

References

Angyal, A. *Foundations for a science of personality.* New York: Commonwealth Fund, 1941.

Badger, E. D. A mother's training program—The road to a purposeful existence. *Children,* 1971, **18** (5), 168-173.

Badger, E. D. The mother's training program—Implementing a home start model in Parent-and-Child Centers. *Children,* March-April, 1972.

Bennett, E. L., Diamond, M. C., Krech, D., & Rosenzweig, M. R. Chemical and anatomical plasticity of the brain. *Science,* 1964, **146** (3644), 610-619.

Bloom, B. S. *Stability and change in human characteristics.* New York: Wiley, 1964.

Brattgård, S. O. The importance of adequate stimulation for the chemical composition of retinal ganglion cells during early postnatal development. *Acta Radiologica,* 1952, Suppl. 96, 1-80.

Conant, J. B. *On understanding science.* New Haven: Yale University Press, 1947. (Mentor Books, 1951, No. 68.)

Dunn, L. C. *A short history of genetics.* New York: McGraw-Hill, 1965.

Ferguson, G. A. On transfer and the abilities of man. *Canadian Journal of Psychology,* 1956, **10**, 121-131.

Ferguson, G. A. Learning and human ability: A theoretical approach. In P. H. DuBois, W. H. Manning, & C. J. Spies (Eds.), *Factor analysis and related techniques in the study of learning.* Technical Report No. 7, Office of Naval Research Contract No. Nonr 816 (02), 1959.

Gagné, R. M., & Paradise, N. E. Abilities and learning sets in knowledge acquisition. *Psychological Monographs,* 1961, 75 (14, Whole No. 518).

Gesell, A., Halverson, H. M., Thompson, H., Ilg, F. L., Castner, B. M., & Bates, L. *The first five years of life.* New York: Harper, 1940.

Glaser, R. Instructional technology and the measurement of learning outcomes: Some questions. *American Psychologist,* 1963, **18**, 519-521.

Glaser, R., & Nitko, A. J. In R. L. Thorndike (Ed.), *Educational measurement.* (2nd ed.) Washington, D.C.: American Council on Education, 1971.

Green, B. F. A method of scalogram analysis using summary statistics. *Psychometrika,* 1966, **21**, 79-88.

Greenberg, D., Uzgiris, I. C., & Hunt, J. McV. Hastening the development of the blink-response with looking. *Journal of Genetic Psychology,* 1968, **113**, 167-176.

Greenberg, D. J., Uzgiris, I. C., & Hunt, J. McV. Attentional preference and experience: III. Visual familiarity and looking time. *Journal of Genetic Psychology,* 1970, **117**, 123-135.

Guilford, J. P. *The nature of human intelligence.* New York: McGraw-Hill, 1967.

Hebb, D. O. *The organization of behavior.* New York: Wiley, 1949.

Hirsch, J. Behavior-genetic analysis and its biosocial consequences. *Seminars in Psychiatry,* 1970, **2**, 89-105.

Humphreys, L. G. The nature and organization of human abilities. In

M. Katz (Ed.), *The 19th yearbook of the National Council on Measurement in Education.* Ames, Iowa, 1962. (a)

Humphreys, L. G. The organization of human abilities. *American Psychologist,* 1962, 17, 475-483. (b)

Hunt, J. McV. Experience and the development of motivation: Some reinterpretations. *Child Development,* 1960, 31, 489-504.

Hunt, J. McV. *Intelligence and experience.* New York: Ronald Press, 1961.

Hunt, J. McV. Piaget's observations as a source of hypotheses concerning motivation. *Merrill-Palmer Quarterly,* 1963, 9, 263-275. (a)

Hunt, J. McV. Motivation inherent in information processing and action. In O. J. Harvey (Ed.), *Motivation and social interaction: The cognitive determinants.* New York: Ronald Press, 1963. (b)

Hunt, J. McV. Intrinsic motivation and its role in psychological development. In D. Levine (Ed.), *Nebraska symposium on motivation.* Vol. 13. Lincoln: University of Nebraska Press, 1965.

Hunt, J. McV. Toward a theory of guided learning in development. In R. H. Ojemann & K. Pritchett (Eds.), *Giving emphasis to guided learning.* Cleveland: Educational Research Council, 1966.

Hunt, J. McV. *The challenge of incompetence and poverty: Papers on the role of early education.* Urbana: University of Illinois Press, 1969.

Hunt, J. McV. Attentional preference and experience: I. Introduction. *Journal of Genetic Psychology,* 1970, 117, 99-107.

Hunt, J. McV. Intrinsic motivation: Information and circumstance. In H. M. Schroder & P. Suedfeld (Eds.), *Personality theory and information processing.* New York: Ronald Press, 1971. (a)

Hunt, J. McV. Intrinsic motivation and psychological development. In H. M. Schroder & P. Suedfeld (Eds.), *Personality theory and information processing.* New York: Ronald Press, 1971. (b)

Hunt, J. McV. Parent and child centers: Their basis in the behavioral and educational sciences. *American Journal of Orthopsychiatry,* 1971, 41 (1), 13-38. (c)

Hunt, J. McV., & Uzgiris, I. C. Cathexis from recognitive familiarity: An exploratory study. In P. R. Merrifield (Ed.), *Experimental and factor-analytic measurement of personality: Contributions by students of J. P. Guilford.* Kent, Ohio: Kent State University Press, 1964.

Katz, P., & Zigler, E. Self-image disparity: A developmental approach. *Journal of Personality and Social Psychology,* 1967, 5, 186-195.

Kohlberg, L., & Zigler, E. The impact of cognitive maturity on the development of sex-role attitudes in the years 4 to 8. *Genetic Psychology Monographs,* 1967, 75, 89-165.

Krech, D., Rosenzweig, M. R., & Bennett, E. L. Environmental impoverishment, social isolation, and changes in brain chemistry and anatomy. *Physiology and Behavior,* 1966, **1**, 99-104.

Paraskevopoulos, J., & Hunt, J. McV. Object construction and imitation under differing conditions of rearing. *Journal of Genetic Psychology,* 1971, **119** (Pt. 2), 301-322.

Piaget, J. *The origins of intelligence in children.* Translated by Margaret Cook. New York: International Universities Press, 1952.

Piaget, J. *The construction of reality in the child.* Translated by Margaret Cook. New York: Basic Books, 1954.

Popham, W. J., & Husek, T. R. Implications of criterion-referenced measurement. *Journal of Educational Measurement,* 1969, **6** (1), 1-9.

Riesen, A. H. The development of visual perception in man and chimpanzee. *Science,* 1947, **106**, 107-108.

Riesen, A. H. Plasticity of behavior: Psychological aspects. In H. F. Harlow & C. N. Woolsey (Eds.), *Biological and biochemical bases of behavior.* Madison: University of Wisconsin Press, 1958.

Schultz, T. R., & Zigler, E. Emotional concomitants of visual mastery in infants: The effects of stimulus movement on, smiling and vocalizing. *Journal of Experimental Psychology,* 1971, **10**, 390-403.

Shirley, M. M. A motor sequence favors the maturation theory. *Psychological Bulletin,* 1931, **28**, 204-205.

Thurstone, L. L. *Primary mental abilities.* Chicago: University of Chicago Press, 1938.

Uzgiris, I. C., & Hunt, J. McV. An instrument for assessing infant psychological development. Mimeographed paper, Psychological Development Laboratory, University of Illinois, 1966.

Uzgiris, I. C. & Hunt, J. McV. Ordinal scales of infant psychological development: Information concerning six demonstration films. Mimeographed paper, Psychological Development Laboratory, University of Illinois, 1968.

Uzgiris, I. C., & Hunt, J. McV. Attentional preference and experience: II. An exploratory longitudinal study of the effects of visual familiarity and responsiveness. *Journal of Genetic Psychology,* 1970, **117**, 109-122.

Valverde, F. Apical dendritic spines of the visual cortex and light deprivation in the mouse. *Experimental Brain Research,* 1967, **3**, 337-352.

Valverde, F. Structural changes in the area striata of the mouse after enucleation. *Experimental Brain Research,* 1968, **5**, 274-292.

Valverde, F., & Esteban, M. E. Peristriate cortex of mouse: Location and the effects of enucleation on the number of dendritic spines. *Brain Research,* 1968, **9**, 145-148.

Watson, J. S. The development and generalization of "contingency awareness" in early infancy: Some hypotheses. *Merrill-Palmer Quarterly of Behavior and Development,* 1966, **12** (2), 123-135.

Watson, J. S. Memory and "contingency analysis" in infant learning.

Merrill-Palmer Quarterly of Behavior and Development, 1967, **13** (1), 55-76.

Weizmann, F., Cohen, L., & Pratt, J. Novelty, familiarity, and the development of infant attention. *Developmental Psychology,* 1971, **4** (2), 149-154.

White, B. L. An experimental approach to the effects of experience on early human development. In J. P. Hill (Ed.), *Minnesota Symposia on Child Development.* Minneapolis: University of Minnesota Press, 1967.

White, B. L. An analysis of excellent early educational practices: Preliminary report. *Interchange,* 1971, **2** (2), 71-88.

White, R. W. Motivation reconsidered: The concept of competence. *Psychological Review,* 1959, **66**, 297-333.

Whorf, B. L. *Language, thought, and reality.* New York: Wiley, 1956.

Wiesel, T. N., & Hubel, D. H. Effects of visual deprivation on morphology and physiology of cells in the cat's lateral geniculate body. *Journal of Neurophysiology,* 1963, **26**, 978-993.

Yarrow, L. J., Rubenstein, J. L., & Pedersen, F. A. Dimensions of early stimulation: Differential effects on infant development. Paper presented at the meetings of the Society for Research in Child Development, Minneapolis, Minn., April 1971.

Zigler, E., Levine, J., & Gould, L. Cognitive challenge as a factor in children's humor appreciation. *Journal of Personality and Social Psychology,* 1967, **6**, 332-336.

Richard P. Toister

Some Applied and Theoretical Implications of Behavior Technology for Mental Retardation

IN RECENT YEARS we have witnessed the successful application of learning theory principles to a wide variety of developmental problems including mental retardation (Bijou, 1968; Nawas & Braun, 1971; W. I. Gardner, 1971). The problems of the retarded are diverse, and subsequently behavior modifiers have dealt with a wide range of developmental skills including: toilet training (Azrin & Foxx, 1971), feeding skills (Berkowitz, Sherry, & Davis, 1971), ambulation (Loynd & Barclay, 1970), speech and language (Sloane & MacAulay, 1968), cognitive behaviors (Hammerlynck & Clark, 1971), as well as social and educational performance (Ramp & Hopkins, 1971). The vast increase in published reports of behavior modification studies with the retarded, of which the previous list is but a small sample, attests to a rapidly developing technology of behavior change. This discussion will not review the dialectics of behavior modification or present a detailed analysis of specific applications to the retarded. Rather, I will outline some of what I feel are important programmatic and theoretical implications of behavioral technology for the field of mental or developmental retardation. The interested reader should

Richard P. Toister, Ph.D., is an assistant professor in the Department of Pediatrics, University of Miami School of Medicine.

consult those texts and references cited previously for more detailed descriptions of behavior modification as applied to problems of the retarded.

Applied Implications

The Antecedent-Consequent Equation

Many attempts have been made at conceptualizing a reinforcement theory approach to applied behavior change yet all have a basic formula in common. For example, O. R. Lindsley (1964) suggested the "A-B-C model" where antecedent-behavioral-consequent events are functionally related in behavioral descriptions. However, whatever notation is used, the basic relations between discriminative stimuli (S^D), responses (behavior), and reinforcers (S^R) as outlined by Skinner (1953) remain the fundamental paradigm in a functional approach. The implications of the so-called A-B-C model are very important for all workers with the retarded whether they be cottage parents or educators. The first major implication is that one must empirically and carefully observe and chart all three events rather than react to "labels" or anecdotal descriptions of behavior. Everyone who has attempted to change behavior in a group or in a one-to-one situation will appreciate the difficulty of describing valid functional relations that lead to positive program changes. The A-B-C paradigm, however, does provide a framework for describing and recording relevant events in applied behavior change provided one carefully and operationally defines all three factors in the equation.

The Teaching Orientation

The three part relation underscores the behavior modifier's reliance on diagnostic teaching rather than diagnostic testing. This implication of the behavioral position has often been misunderstood by professionals and workers in the field. The implication is not, from my point of view, that intellectual evaluations are superfluous but that in many situations they do not accurately pinpoint deficit behaviors so as to lead to remedial efforts. Theoretical controversy aside, "intelligent" is still an adjective and as such only describes a person's standing relative to his peers on certain behavioral items without specifying what events are necessary to change any deficit behaviors identified. Diagnostic evaluations are viewed as a first general step in program development to the extent that certain scores may indicate the relative deficits one individual demonstrates within his behavioral repertoire compared with his peers.

"Nothing Accelerates Learning Like Teaching"

The quotation by R. G. Buddenhagen (1971) used for the subhead above surmises the third consideration for the A-B-C paradigm. The third implication of the A-B-C paradigm is that "the organism is always right." That is, the failure of an individual to learn may be the function of an inadequate or inaccurate program (given that individual's unique genetic, biological, and environmental history) rather than an unalterable deficit or defect within the individual. Thus, when goals are not achieved, the behavior analyst emphasizes changing procedures rather than labeling or rejecting individuals. This general position has been stated many times and in many ways but is perhaps best expressed in a recent paper by W. A. Bricker (1970):

> Finally, I wish to affirm my belief in the importance of the nervous system and to indicate a conviction that a host of events can do damage to it and to its functioning. However, only the failure of a perfectly valid, perfectly reliable, efficient program of training will convince me that the identification of the deficit is sufficient reason to stop trying to educate the child. Somehow, I cannot feel that we have reached perfection in the development of training programs.

Consequently, in remedial education, for example, today's teacher with appropriate training can produce predictable and positive behavior change and need no longer be impatient with a retarded child but with a procedure. In a behaviorally oriented program a child is not labeled or rejected but an ineffective program is identified and altered in reference to given behavior(s). Thus, retarded individuals are no longer constrained by a priori estimates of ability, but rather are led step by step to specified goals as defined by individual programs. Indeed this orientation has led some bold behavior modifiers to suggest that we are now ready to approach the teaching of "love" and "joy" (Homme et al., 1968).

Who Does What?

A final but very important implication of behavior technology for the retarded is the capability of placing increased responsibility for effective intervention into the hands of such paraprofessionals and nonprofessionals as parents and peers (J. M. Gardner, 1970; Wahler, 1970). Recent studies, such as those just cited and others (Toister et al., 1968), have demonstrated that with training and supervision various so-called behavior technicians can effect significant positive changes in behavior whether in residential or outpatient environments. As a result it is becoming more feasible to envision program designs where such services are pyramided so as to reach a majority of individuals with atypical and deficit behaviors (Tharp & Wetzel, 1969) with a concomitant saving in professional time and program cost. Such behavior change teams have the long-range potential of making rather significant and long-lasting inroads into the problems of the retarded now without waiting for dramatic new developments in prevention or treatment.

Theoretical Implications

Epistomology

The question of how man attains knowledge of the world has intrigued both philosophers and scientists from Plato to Piaget. Itard was convinced that he had but to write with the pen of experience on the *tabla rasa* of the Savage of Aveyron to make the unfortunate boy normal. The philosophical empiricism of Locke and Hume was not dramatically confirmed in Itard's experiment, but he did change some of the child's behavior and in that sense he "knew" more of the world. Contemporary theories, whether the genetic epistomology of Jean Piaget or the behavioral epistomology of B. F. Skinner, will someday have to relate to biologic epistomology (John, 1972) as neurophysiologists come closer and closer to the biochemical description of brain function in relation to environmental events. Nevertheless, on a behavioral level, if one accepts some of the theoretical implications of a reinforcement analysis with the retarded, the intriguing possibility that "to know one must behave" opens new vistas in the very difficult analysis of man "thinking." The possibilities of Skinner's *Verbal Behavior* (1957) have yet to be even partially studied as these relate to the problem of aiding retarded individuals in so-called higher cognitive functioning. Some studies (e.g., Guess, 1969) suggest that by carefully arranging contingencies grammatical abstractions can be taught to lower level retarded children. Itard, interestingly enough, reported similar observations, but he met with less success when he attempted to teach such speech to his pupil. Yet, recent work with animals (Premack, 1971) suggests that contingent environmental programming can produce complex verbal behavior, such as class concepts, class names, and conditional relations in chimpanzees. Again, the theoretical implications are quite fascinating, namely, that "nature" has not scratched the surface of the many possible contingencies that may result in heretofore unexpected behavioral development. In the very complex area of knowledge and the retarded, behavior technology certainly poses challenging possibilities to interested investigators who are prepared for hard, diligent, and tedious research. However, the long-range potential of discovering contingencies for improving the "thinking" of retarded individuals more than compensates for the expenditure of effort.

Motivation

The concept of motive is central to almost all theories or explanations of behavior. The published literature is replete with labels for explaining the why of behavior, including such terms as needs, motives, press, *trieb* (drive), desires, instincts, propensities, traits, forces, valences, and so on (Madsen, 1961). Yet in dealing with the problems of changing the behavior of the retarded, for instance, we do not change any of these. What we can alter are environmental events, such as verbal praise or reproof, stars or checks on a chart, marks on paper, pats on the back, and contingent M & Ms (the candy or psychological kind) to name a few. The major theoretical implication, although it may sound trite at this stage of the game, is that to move or change behavior we must look to the external environment. The consequence of following the theoretical implications of the concept of a reinforcement analysis with the retarded has been the rapid development of new approaches to old problems (e.g., Sidman and Stoddard, 1966). Specifically, rather than looking to defects or deficits in needs, drives, or instincts to answer motivational questions, one must specify the variables or contingencies of which retarded behavior is a function. This simple but important implication is often overlooked in applied and basic research studies with the retarded and one can still hear such terms as unmotivated or lazy being used to explain why a retarded individual does not perform in a given instance. In other words, it may not be a lack of concern for approval but the lack of approval itself, past and present, which suppresses performances.

A Note of Caution

The foregoing should not be interpreted to mean that behavior technology is a panacea for the problems of the retarded. All too often the claims and promises of enthusiastic behavior modifiers veil the hard and careful work involved in the development and application of a functional program. No one should confuse success of behavioral technology with ease of implementation without talking to numerous technicians, teachers, parents, and graduate students. The application of behavior principles requires hard, tedious effort under the direction of well-trained personnel. Frequently and sadly, I have observed so-called behavior modification programs where ill-trained staff fully identified the technology with "giving an M & M." The lesson is clear—giving M & Ms is not necessarily behavior modification.

Finally, I would like to suggest that even the most experienced worker in the field of retardation cannot fully appreciate the day-to-day frustration, failure, and unintentional indifference that confront most retarded individuals in even the most benevolent environments. Yet, concern and sympathy will not necessarily help such individuals to better their lot in today's complex world. Such concern should be translated into valid, reliable, and effective programs of intervention. Although a behavioral technology may not be a panacea, it certainly offers the potential for radically and positively changing the lives of many thousands of those "creatures ill-favored of nature, rejected by society and abandoned by medicine," to quote Itard.

References

Azrin, N. H., & Foxx, R. M. A rapid method of toilet training the institutionalized retarded. *Journal of Applied Behavior Analysis,* 1971, 89-99.

Berkowitz, S., Sherry, P. J., & Davis, B. Teaching self-help feeding skills to profound retardates using reinforcement and fading procedures. *Behavior Therapy,* 1971, 2, 62-67.

Bijou, S. W. Behavior modification in the mentally retarded. *Pediatric Clinics of North America,* 1968, 15, 969-987.

Bricker, W. A. Identifying and modifying behavioral deficits. *American Journal of Mental Deficiency,* 1970, 75, 16-21.

Buddenhagen, R. G. *Establishing vocal verbalizations in mute mongoloid children.* Champaign, Ill.: Research Press, 1971.

Gardner, J. M. Differential effectiveness of two methods for teaching behavior modification techniques to institutional attendants. Paper presented at the 94th meeting of the American Association on Mental Deficiency, 1970.

Gardner, W. I. *Behavior modification in mental retardation.* Chicago: Aldine, 1971.

Guess, D. A functional analysis of receptive language and productive speech: acquisition of the plural morpheme. *Journal of Applied Behavior Analysis,* 1969, 2, 55-64.

Hammerlynck, L. A., & Clark, F. W. (Eds.) *Behavior modification for exceptional children and youth.* Calgary, Canada: J. D. McAra, Ltd., 1971.

Homme, L., C'DeBaca, P., Cottingham, L., & Homme, A. What behavioral engineering is. *The Psychological Record*, 1968, **18**, 425-434.

John, E. R. Switchboard versus statistical theories of learning and memory. *Science*, 1972, **177**, 850-864.

Lindsley, O. R. Direct measurement and prosthesis of retarded behavior. *Journal of Education*, 1964, **147**, 62-81.

Loynd, J., & Barclay, A. A case study in developing ambulation in a profoundly retarded child. *Journal of Behavior Research and Therapy*, 1970, **8**, 207.

Madsen, K. B. *Theories of motivation*. Cleveland: Howard Allen, Inc., 1961.

Nawas, M. M., & Braun, S. H. The use of operant techniques for modifying the behavior of the severely and profoundly retarded. Part I. Introduction and initial phase. *Mental Retardation*, 1971, **8**, 2-6.

Premack, D. Language in chimpanzee? *Science*, 1971, **172**, 808-822.

Ramp, E. A., & Hopkins, B. L. *A new direction for education*. Vol. 1. *Behavior analysis*. University of Kansas, Department of Human Development, 1971.

Sidman, M., & Stoddard, L. T. Programming perception for retarded. In N. Ellis (Ed.), *International review of research in mental retardation*. Vol. 2. New York: Academic Press, 1966.

Skinner, B. F. *Science and human behavior*. New York: Macmillan, 1953.

Sloane, H. N., & MacAulay, B. D. (Eds.) *Operant procedures in remedial speech and language training*. Boston: Houghton Mifflin, 1968.

Tharp, R. G., & Wetzel, R. J. *Behavior modification in the natural environment*. New York: Academic Press, 1969.

Toister, R. P., Pesek, S., Bell, B., & Soulary, E. Training parents of severely retarded pre-school children in behavior management techniques. Unpublished paper, University of Miami, 1968.

Wahler, R. G. Peers as classroom behavior modifiers. Paper presented at the 94th meeting of the American Association on Mental Deficiency, 1970.

Index

Adamo, C. C., 96
Adaptive Behavior Check List, 94, 98
Adler, D., 70
Allen, R. M., 54, 87, 90. 96, 107
alternate elaboration retardation, 80
Angyal, A., 131
antecedent-consequent equation, A-B-C model, 150
anxious retardates, 61
Aschenbach, T., 21, 23, 24, 25, 29
Azrin, H., 151

Badger, E. D., 141, 142
Balla, D., 28, 35
Bandura, A., 76
Baratz, J. C., 73
Barclay, A., 149
Barnes, R. H., 76
Bayley, N., 128, 132
behavior modification, applied implications, 149
Bennett, E. L., 130
Berkowitz, S., 149
Bernard, J. S., 64
Bernstein, B., 72, 73
Biber, B., 79
Bijou, S. W., 149
Bloom, B. S., 73, 131
border-line retardation, 58
Boutourline-Young, H., 75
Brattgård, S. O., 130
Braun, S. H., 149
Bricker, W. A., 151
Bruner, J. S., 21, 37, 38, 47
Buddenhagen, R. G., 151
Burks, B. S., 33
Butterfield, E. C., 20, 25, 28, 68, 69

Canaday, H. B., 68
chronological age, relation to mental age and IQ, 13-27
Clark, F. W., 149
cognitive difference theory, 14
Cohen, L., 125
Cole, M., 69
competence and effectence, 128
Conant, J. B., 132
Cortazzo, A. D., 37, 90, 96, 107
Couture, A. E., 101
Cravioto, J., 77
criterion-referenced test, 133
Cruse, D., 31

Davies, S. P., 30

Davis, B., 149
Deblinger, J., 70
deprivation retardation, 72
developmental considerations, 76-81
developmental stages (Piaget), 39
Developmental Test of Visual Perception, Mariane Frostig, 53
Development and Training Division, 92, 105
Diamond, M. C., 130
difference orientation, 13
Diggory, J. C., 30
divisional concept, the new horizontally structured institution, 89, 90, 91
Douvan, E., 75
Dunn, L., 89, 136, 138

Edgerton, R. B., 31
Education and Training Division, 93, 101
Einsteinian model man, 44, 48
Elkind, D., 38, 57, 68, 70, 79
Elkstein, R., 76
enactive, ikonic, and symbolic modes, 37ff.
Estaban, M. E., 130

Ferguson, G. A., 125
Flavell, J., 40
Fleming, E. S., 70
Forrester, B. J., 68
Foshee, J. G., 14
Foxx, R. M., 149
Freud, S., 78
Frostig, M., 53

Gagne, R. M., 133
Gardner, B., 41, 43, 46
Gardner, W. I., 149
genetic endowment, 67
Gesell, A., 122, 135
Glaser, R., 133
Goldstein, H., 31
Goldstein, K., 14
Goodnow, J., 74
Gordon, I. J., 41, 44, 48, 49
Gould, L., 126
Green, B. F., 134
Green, C., 17
Greenberg, D. J., 125, 136,
Greenfield, P. M., 74
Guess, D. A., 153
Guilford, J. P., 44, 133

Hammerlynck, L. A., 149
Head Start Program, 68
Hebb, D. O., 130
heredity, 39
Hermelin, B., 14
Hernnstein, R., 67
Hess, R. D., 72
HIP evaluation, 94
Hirsch, J., 139
Hodgen, L., 17
Homme, L., 152
Hopkins, B. L., 149
Hospital Improvement Project (HIP), 87-89
Hottel, J. V., 30
House, B. J., 14
Hubel, D. H., 130
Humphreys, L. G., 124, 125, 131
Hunt, J. McV., 38, 44, 48, 121, 123, 124, 125, 126, 128, 131, 134, 136, 140
Husek, T. R., 135
Hyden, H., 130

Illinois Test of Psycholinguistic Abilities, 53
Independent Living Division, 92, 103
intellectual deprivation retardation, 72
intelligence: developmental, homeostatic, and monolothic views, 41ff.
intelligence concepts revisited, 125ff.
IQ, as a concept, 122; in relation to mental and chronological ages, 13-27

Irons, N., 28
Itard, J., 9, 152, 153

Jacobsen, L., 70
Jensen, A. R., 67
John, E. R., 153
Johnson, G. O., 31
Jones, H. E., 32

Katz, P., 126
Kirk, S. A., 31
Klaus, R. A., 68
Kohlberg, L., 127,
Kounin, J., 14
Krech, D., 130

Leahy, A. M., 33
learning principles, 49
Lennenberg, H., 81
Levine J., 126
Lewin, K., 14
liberated retardates, 60
Lindsley, O. R., 150
Long, E., 71
longitudinal validity factors, 130
Lott, A. J., 75
Lott, B. E., 75
low income retardates, 62
Loynd, J., 149
Lucito, L. J., 30
Luria, A. R., 14

MacAulay, B. D., 149
Madsen, K. B., 154
maturation and experience, 129-30
measurement strategies revised, 132-36
mental age, relation to chronological age and IQ, 13-27
Mermelstein, E., 74
Metera Baby Centre, 137
middle income retardated, 59
motivation, 153
motivational and interpersonal deprivation retardation, 75
motivational autonomy, 127
motivational difference theory, 15
Municipal Orphanage, 137
Mussen, P., 75

Nawas, M. M., 149
negativistic adolescent retardation, 63
Newtonian model man, 44
Nitko, A. J., 133
norm-referenced test, 133
nutritional deprivational retardation, 76

O'Connor, N., 14
outer-directedness phenomenon, 16, 31

Paradise, N. E., 133
Paraskevopoulos, J., 125, 140
Parent-and-Child Center, 137
Pedersen, F. A., 128
Peluffo, N., 74
Penrose, L., 32
Piaget, J., 38, 39, 40, 45, 47, 136, 137, 138, 152, 153
Piagetian tasks, 74
Popham, W. J., 134,
Pratt, J., 125
Premack, D., 153
premature structured retardation, 78
psychological development, ordinal scales of, 134

Ramp, E. A., 149
Riesen, A. H., 130
Robinson, H., 39 40
Rosen, M., 30, 132
Rosenthal, R., 70
Rosenzweig, M. R., 130,
Rubenstein, 128

Sabagh, G., 31
Sanders, B., 20, 25, 26, 28
Schickedanz, D., 137
Schultz, T. R., 126

Schwartz, B. J., 87, 101
Seeley, H. B., 7
Sequin, E., 9
Sherry, P. J., 149
Shipman, V. C., 72
Shirley, M., 134
Sidman, M., 154
Siegel, P. S., 14, 31
Sigel, I. E., 74
Skinner, B. F., 150, 153
Sloane, H. N., 149
Smyth, P. M., 76
Spearman, C., 133
Spitz, H. H., 14
Stern, W., 122
Stevenson, H. W., 17
Stock, M. B., 76
Stoddard, C. T., 154,
Strother, S., 52

Terman, L. M., 122
Tharp, E. G., 152
theoretical implications of behavior modification, 152
theories of test retardation, limited genetic endowment, 66-72
Thurstone, L. L., 133
Toister, R. P., 149
Tolman, E. C., 21
traditional or vertically structured institutions, 88
transaction and cognitive development, 37
Turnure, J. E., 18, 24, 29, 31
Tyler, F., 47

Urbano, P., 75
Uzgiris, I. C., 125, 126, 128, 131, 134, 136

Valverde, F., 130
Vernon, P. E., 74
Vocational Rehabilitation Division, 93, 99

Wahler, R. G., 152
Walters, B. H., 76
Watson, J. S., 128
Weizmann, F., 125
Werlinsky, B., 30
Wetzel, R. J., 152
White, B. L., 128, 131, 136
White, R. W., 38, 128
Whorf, B. L., 121
Wiesel, T. N., 130

Yando, R., 24, 25, 27, 28, 29
Yarrow, L. J., 128, 132

Zeaman, D., 14
Zigler, E., 13, 17, 20, 24, 25, 27, 28, 29, 32, 38, 68, 69, 126, 127